Cutting and Pasting Truth

PRAISE FOR
CUTTING AND PASTING TRUTH

"I love the fact that God does not expect us to navigate this journey called "life" alone. He makes us all family so we can live life together. In her candid, challenging, and often humorous style, Meredith encourages us to press on, keep the faith, and enjoy the process of becoming all that we were created to be. This isn't just her story or her opinion. *Cutting and Pasting Truth* is infused with the Word of God from start to finish. I loved this book, and you will too."

—**Terry Meeuwsen,** Co-host, *The 700 Club*, Founder of Orphan's Promise

"Cutting and Pasting Truth is for the reader who experiences debilitating pain and scars from emotional wounds. Bunting's unique ability to see humor in all situations and her sole ability to express herself will leave readers chuckling. More importantly, this book opens readers' eyes to the unfailing love of Jesus."

—**Beverly DeVries**, Ed.D., Professor Emerita, Speaker, and Author of
twelve academic books

"Whether you read for inspiration, encouragement, spiritual growth, or purely for pleasure, *Cutting and Pasting Truth* delivers it all. Meredith Bunting seamlessly combines personal stories with biblical accounts, adding thought-provoking Bible verses that need no explanation. She writes with wisdom and emotion and sprinkles just enough humor to keep a smile on your face."

—**Crystal Bowman,** Award-Winning, Best-Selling Author of more than
100 books for women, children, and families

"Bunting uses phrases we've never read before; her discoveries resonate for all of us; she shares daily living as sacred acts."

—**Dr. Robert Christin,** 1921–2013

CUTTING
AND
PASTING
TR U TH

SNAPSHOTS OF A LIFE LIVED
THROUGH FAITH & FITNESS

meredith
bunting

NASHVILLE

NEW YORK • LONDON • MELBOURNE • VANCOUVER

Cutting and Pasting Truth

Snapshots of a Life Lived Through Faith and Fitness

© 2022 Meredith Bunting

Published in New York, New York, by Morgan James Publishing. Morgan James is a trademark of Morgan James, LLC. www.MorganJamesPublishing.com

Proudly distributed by Ingram Publisher Services.

Unless otherwise indicated, all Scripture quotations are from The ESV® Bible (The Holy Bible, English Standard Version®), copyright © 2001 by Crossway, a publishing ministry of Good News Publishers. Used by permission. All rights reserved. Scripture quotations marked "NIV" are taken from the New International Version®, NIV®. Copyright © 1973, 1978, 1984, 2011 by Biblica, Inc.™ Used by permission of Zondervan. Scripture quotations marked "MSG" are taken from The Message. Copyright 1993, 1994, 1995, 1996, 2000, 2001, 2002.

Morgan James BOGO™

A **FREE** ebook edition is available for you or a friend with the purchase of this print book.

_____

CLEARLY SIGN YOUR NAME ABOVE

Instructions to claim your free ebook edition:
1. Visit MorganJamesBOGO.com
2. Sign your name CLEARLY in the space above
3. Complete the form and submit a photo of this entire page
4. You or your friend can download the ebook to your preferred device

ISBN 9781631956447 paperback
ISBN 9781631956454 ebook
Library of Congress Control Number:
2021938724

Cover Design by:
Rachel Lopez
www.r2cdesign.com

Interior Design by:
Christopher Kirk
www.GFSstudio.com

Interior Image Illustrator:
Carol Heischober

Morgan James is a proud partner of Habitat for Humanity Peninsula and Greater Williamsburg. Partners in building since 2006.

Get involved today! Visit MorganJamesPublishing.com/giving-back

To you, Gramma Rene in Heaven, I dedicate this book.

TABLE OF CONTENTS

ACKNOWLEDGMENTS

This is my favorite part of the book, thanking those of you who have encouraged me along this writing adventure and given me the courage to get *Cutting and Pasting Truth* published. You are the ones who carried the scissors and gallons of glue so my stories could tell the truth loud and clear.

It was my father's mother, Irene, who told me with the kindest of eyes, "God is Love." Her words carried me over the years, straight to Jesus, when they became truth for God's story in mine. To you, Gramma Rene in Heaven, I dedicate this book.

All three of our daughters have given me exactly what I've needed at the perfect time to offer this book to an audience. They have been ceaseless in prayer for me since they were little girls in my lap. Each of them has a place in my heart, which I will carry to Heaven.

Robin, you have always been my most ardent cheerleader. How could I ever quit anything while you applauded and claimed to the world how amazing I am? I remember the evening at the dinner table when you announced, "Well, I think we have an aerobics teacher in the family!" as if a new genetic strain had been discovered. Thank you for pushing me so enthusiastically and never letting me quit.

Kerith, your faith in me is passionate, your devotional letter for my seventy-fifth birthday being the perfect expression of your love. I would still be in a pit of despair if not for your prayers for peace, hope, and victory through my episodes of conflict, doubt, and pain, along with the usual whining. At every turn, you met me with truth—"Mom. God is good, always so good." Thank you for praying my book into reality.

Leslie, my text taskmaster, and tour guide, you have always kept me correct and on the right road with no excuses. Whether it be my questionable habits, excessive commas, or elementary knowledge of art museums, you have been honest and unyielding because you are smarter than your mother, and you expect her to be the best at everything. Thank you for editing as many of my faults as possible, loving me despite them, and allowing me a few of my own commas along the way.

The father and hero of our three is my loving husband and valiant friend, who has cheered me on in this writing endeavor through my angst, nerves, tears, and misspelled words. Dan, thank you for your love, encouragement, and faith in me. You are the greatest blessing in my life.

All ten of our grandchildren—Alec, Gabriel, Josselyn, Sadie, Childers, Meredith, Hunter, Elizabeth, Audrey, and Knox—have given me a reason to keep on writing because their stories teach me the joys of life and the supreme honor of being, "MomMom" ("MomBomb" to Knox). I adore you and leave you this book as your legacy of sorts.

I want to commend my web designer, Alec Mangum, for creating the unique and compelling web page that has drawn readers to my stories. If you haven't seen it already, take a look—meredithbunting.com; it is a real treat. Alec, thank you for bringing my stories to life. As always, "As you wish!"

Kimberly Malloy, my friend, mentor, counselor, coach, sister-in-Christ, and bigger-than-life inspiration, thank you for telling me in the most loving way, "Quit whining and get to work." Kimberly, you just have a way with words. My job is done. Now, it is time for yours!

Beverly DeVries, professor of Literacy and writer of a dozen textbooks, could have just blown me off when I asked her to read my unedited stories. Instead of scoffing, she celebrated the possibility of a book in the future. Beverly, your encouragement, wisdom, and love made my dream come true! Thank you for all your prayers, cards, and gifts that make a friendship made in heaven tangible and so much fun on earth.

Thank you, Carol Heischober, my indefatigable art teacher and mentor, for sharing your precious memories of Erin with me and reminding me to treasure every moment I have with my daughters. Enhancing this book are sketches from your beautiful heart.

I will always be indebted to Sharon Poch for insisting twenty years ago that I join her writing class. That Memoirs class was taught by the venerable Dr. Robert Christen who made me cry when he told me I truly was a writer. Sharon, thank you for always believing in me and pointing the way.

Pastor Nate Atwood was the first to inspire me to write devotionals for our church. A few years later, he introduced me to Ernie Vanderwilt, a giant-hearted man who became my cohort for spiritual writing, when we sought the LORD for wisdom, truth, and inspiration to share in our devotionals. These two men of God led me to ". . . address my verses to the King." (Psalm 45:1)

Never in my days did I think I would be thanking a publishing company for accepting my book. But I sure prayed about it. Morgan James Publishers, I believe you are the answer to my prayers, and "my cup runneth over!" From professionalism to prayer, every detail of the publishing process has been handled with integrity and support. I'm especially grateful to Chris and Jim Howard to whom Sherry Pinkerton, fellow writer, speaker, and podcaster ("Finding God in Your Pain"), introduced me, for their gracious hospitality and encouragement right from the beginning. Morgan James, you are an amazing team!

My editor has been the ribbon wrapped around all the scattered pages of my manuscript as I learned how to navigate through the Internet. With a ready laugh, hearty encouragement, long-suffering patience, and experienced wisdom, Cortney Donelson made a daunting task into a fun adventure. From the first word to the last, I've known Cortney has had my back. Cortney, I am blessed to call you "friend," and I thank you with my whole heart. I will never be afraid of editors again!

And to you Jesus, my LORD and Savior, with the Psalmist I sing:

Behold, You delight in truth in the inward being,
and You teach me wisdom in the secret heart. (Psalm 51:6)

Thank you for giving me Your words of Truth for my story. Amen

FOREWORD

eing asked to write the forward for someone's book is like being invited to the delivery room for the birth of a child. *Cutting and Pasting Truth* is filled with love, pain, heartache, testimonies, deliverance, and transparency. It is an honor and privilege that I write this for Meredith and joyfully encourage you to grab a cup of coffee, pen, highlighter, notepad, or whatever you need to remember the nuggets you will receive on this journey. Meredith is a skilled wordsmith who paints a vivid picture of not only the events in her life but also the emotions that we so often hide behind our masks to appear to have it all together.

I first met Meredith when I spoke at a women's retreat and she introduced the concept of "Godography." As a licensed marriage and family therapist, I am familiar with genograms and the incredible insight they bring to our awareness but had never heard of this idea. I was excited to learn a new perspective on a familiar tool. I went back to my hotel room that night and began at once to write my timeline, this time superimposed where I saw God's story in my life.

Understanding that we are all born with a desire for love and belonging, I saw how I was loved from the moment I was " . . . knit together in my mother's womb" (Psalm 139:13) and how I have always belonged and how my inability to see and understand this had impacted my behaviors.

Meredith knows the Word, knows herself, and is unapologetically authentic with her experiences, guiding us back to Truth time after time. I found myself saying, "me too" many times when she dove into deep waters of emotion from lies she had told herself but was once again refreshed when she poured the healing Word of Truth over her wounds.

Read this book all at once or one chapter at a time. Just be ready to walk away knowing *you* are loved and *you* belong—always have and always will.

Thank you, Meredith, for this gift!

—**Kimberly Malloy,** LMFT, CIO at Center for Relational Health LV, Co-Host at A View From Above, President at Train2excel, Inc.

INTRODUCTION

Before the Hound of Heaven hurled me to my knees, I was a fluff ball. Prone to whimsy and whining, I floated and flitted about without much thought. Figuring things out, grasping a purpose, and trying to settle down were impossible for me. Nothing made sense, and I did not know where I fit into the big picture. I always tried to be good, yet inside, I felt was very, very bad. I lived in fear.

My faith emerged way before I was aware enough to sense it. As a child, the oldest of four siblings, moving from one military base to the next, I made up stories in my head about families that stayed home and had fences around big yards. I fought my fears with fantasy.

My grandmother told me, "God is love." A new idea.

He wasn't to be feared? "God is love." He wasn't mad at how bad I was? "God is love." Would He see me wherever I went? "God is love." Over and over, with the kindest of eyes, my Gramma Rene assured me, "God is love."

With those words in my heart and the tiniest seed of faith born, I moved with my family to Hawaii, oceans away from my beloved grandmother. Alone and stranded with my terrors, I hoped with a ten-year-old's desperation that God knew where I had gone. Did He still love me?

Decades passed, and I learned He does love me, as He loves each of us. This is the truth I found after years of searching, questioning, and almost giving up on any purpose or chance for love. My life—like yours—is a story written by our Creator with truth on every page. We just have to look past our failures, misgivings, and sorrows to see that God not only has been with us all along but has pasted His truths of joy, hope, and love throughout our lives.

If kept in the dark, our stories eat us alive. Empowerment is the by-product of the realization that we have found God, and He has chosen us. When we surrender ourselves to our Creator, the details of our yesterdays become God's glory today. No matter where we go to find Him, He will "make all things new," and He will be exalted!

Then you will call upon Me and come and pray to Me and I will hear you.
You will seek Me and find Me when you seek Me with all your heart.
I will be found by you, declares the Lord . . . (Jeremiah 29:12,14)

The stories in the first section of *Cutting and Pasting Truth* are God's stories from my life as He worked out His plan in me. It is the account of a young woman's faith as God revealed that she was not a Fluff Ball, as she had been called, but a beloved child of her Creator. As I struggled to become an adult—which was a frightening identity—and hang on to my dream to become a mother—the most elusive role of my imagination—God protected me from my fears and myself.

I did become a wife and a mother. But it didn't turn out like I thought it would. I had no role model other than my own conflicted mother and the Puritan-perfect mothers on television shows. I did not know how to be a wife, especially to a Navy fighter pilot, who was gone six months out of the year, and I certainly did not know how to selflessly nurture babies. I was at the end of my rope, which was precisely where God was waiting. "I am Love."

The stories in the second part of this book are about fitness, both physical and spiritual, where God relentlessly interceded in circumstances, to teach me more about Himself and strip away more of myself. It was during this time, from my thirties to my sixties, that I learned the disciplines, challenges, and victories of living life as a Christian—a follower of Jesus. It was God's fitness program, if you will, with His goal not to make me thin but learn to trust in Him.

Oddly enough, as God exercised His will in me, helping me shed fear, pride, and a load of sins, I landed a job at the Founders Inn as manager of their five-star fitness center, owned then by CBN in Virginia Beach. At that time, my husband had a new career in finance, our three daughters were teenagers, I taught aerobic classes. I had never had a salaried job in my life; I didn't even know how to operate a copy machine. But I was given a facility and a staff to manage. God placed me exactly where He wanted me. He had a Plan.

As my career in the health and fitness field grew, I flourished in my management duties and developed a well-toned physically fit body. Living out my mantra, "Movement is life," I felt invincible for a decade.

The truth is, God was more interested in my spiritual fitness than my BMI or working heart rate. It was only through His grace that I was able to cope with changing corporate hierarchy, demands of family life with teenagers, my husband's career change, the needs of our aging mothers, and ultimately, my failing health. I wasn't invincible after all and fell apart as rheumatoid arthritis seared through my joints.

That brings us to the third section of *Cutting and Pasting Truth*, a section filled with bitter honesty about my crucible. I fought God for a long time over my painful disability. It seemed so unfair to have been given the gift of physical fitness and the opportunity to create a fitness ministry to then take a hammer to it. But God knew it was time for me to slow down, get over myself, and learn to press into Him. Kicking and screaming, I finally began to trust Him in my new unwanted season and to just breathe in His love. His words to the Apostle Paul, "My grace is sufficient for you, for my power is made perfect in weakness," (2 Corinthians 12:9) seemed spoken to me also. Actually, they were yelled at me. As C.S. Lewis wrote in my dog-eared, tear-stained book, *The Problem of Pain*, God "shouts to us in our pain; it is His megaphone to a deaf world."

Though my body, which had been so fit and able, is weary and crooked now, my faith in my God who has been with me all the days of my life is deep and strong. I am immersed in the fruit of the Spirit and am abiding in the peace of Jesus Christ, my Savior. My greatest hope is that I will "dwell in the house of the Lord forever" and stand on the truth: "God is love."

The final section of this book is composed of snapshots for every season and holiday. They are glimpses into the work God has been doing inside me during the most memorable parts of my life.

My prayer is that these stories become devotions to encourage and remind you of God's love for you in your story.

SECTION I

FAITH

FINDING GOD IN YOUR STORY

> See, I have engraved you on the palm of my hands,
> your walls are continually before me. (Isaiah 49:16)

Do you see God's handprint on your life? Have you noticed the intervention of the Almighty in a childhood, or perhaps last week's, memory? Take a moment to peruse the pathways of yesteryear. Go ahead, shake your head, laugh out loud, even feel tears as you reminisce the decades of your life. In spite of little white lies, the big bold ones, strange or broken relationships, good and bad decisions, thwarted career paths, sports-obsessed spouses, overdrawn checking accounts, unconventional kids, or three too many pets, your life is sacred. You are God's creation, and His Hand has been upon you.

> But I trust in You, O Lord; I say, "You are my God."
> My times are in Your hand. (Psalm 31: 14, 15a)

Now, look at your hands. Turn them over and gaze into your palms, fingers, and thumbs. This is a hard exercise for me because my hands are crooked and floppy from arthritis. If I made up stories from my fingertips, they would look like cartoons or weird sci-fi! Nevertheless, God has used my hands to hold ten new grandbabies, wipe tears from my daughters' eyes, clap at the children's school programs, tape together 272 paper Easter eggs with my five-year-old granddaughter, walk hand-in-hand along the sidewalk with her, singing songs with made-up words, flip back and forth through the silken pages of my Bible to find just the right passage to read when my mother passed away and to hold my husband's hand, hard, through five decades of marriage.

Is your handprint on someone's life? Who have you put your hands on to comfort, soothe, pat, lift, or carry? These are God stories. Just as you have cared for and protected those you love to the best of your ability, even more so, God has covered you from the moment you were conceived.

Like an open book, you watched me grow from conception to birth;
all the stages of my life were spread out before You, the days of my life
all prepared before I'd even lived one day. (Psalm 139: 16, MSG)

What would be your answer to the question, "Would you live your life over if you could?" Most of us would say, "Well, I guess so. But only if I knew what I know now!" What wonders would unfold if we all looked back to see what God knew all along!

This is why I journal. Right above me, on the shelf over my desk, are dozens of books of different colors, patterns, and sizes. They are filled with the accounts of my days since I began my walk with Jesus. This journey of mine with Him of over forty years is what I am still writing about—the stories have been cut and pasted into this book!

Today I chatted on paper about the satin sunrise, my hopes for the day, my concern for a beloved family, and my gratitude for any opportunity He'll bring my way to know Him better, even if it means inconvenience or discomfort. I still just want His presence!

A couple of years ago, I was in a bad place after a long bout of pain and heavy medication. I struggled in a dark hole of self-pity, exaggerated fears, and unreasonable doubts. I yanked down all my journals with the intention of "tossing away my life." With my trashcan beside me, I flipped through pages of first one journal, then another. Tears, hot and cleansing, streamed as I read over and over my cries to the Lord to deliver, guide, forgive, and be with me. Between my pleas were exclamation points and praise where I read of joys, healings, provision, and answered prayers.

Your testimonies are also my delight and my counselors. (Psalm 119:24)

God rocked my soul by showing me three things. One: All through the years, in spite of all my wails, I'd never stopped loving Him. Two: He loved me right back because He knew my faith (Genesis 15:6). Three: I could trust this God I had written about for years because His testimonies in my life proved His faithfulness.

I dusted off the shelf, reorganized my journals, and placed them where they belonged, just as God had cleaned off the mire in my soul and put me on a high place where I belonged.

You have turned for me my mourning into dancing. You have loosed my sackcloth and clothed me with gladness. (Psalm 30:11)

Evidence of God in the details of your life teaches you about His character. God's provision, presence, blessing, discipline, and even silence are threads of Truth, designing the tapestry of your life. These stories are worth recording, and they are most powerful when shared.

Telling your story from a spiritual perspective honors God, imparts an understanding of His sovereignty, and "is the beginning of wisdom" (Psalm 111:10). Write it down so His testimonies are not forgotten. God will be glorified when you share what you've learned about Him.

"God is faithful!" you will say because your story has been God's story all along.

My heart overflows with a pleasing theme. I address my verses to the King: my tongue is the pen of a ready scribe. (Psalm 45:1)

CUT AND PASTE TRUTH

All mission trips carry with them some risk. Whether serving in a foreign country, in the jungle, down the street, or at the seaside, as I was doing, a mission trip calls for obedience, surrender, and a whole lot of faith. When we go to people to bring them God's message, we cannot rely on one ounce of ourselves. In essence, we are interceding for God into other peoples' stories. We must go with a humble and open heart. We must also work very hard not to show fear.

I went on a mission trip last weekend. Leaving behind my husband, dogs, and birthday grandchildren, along with the garden, tomato plants, and hanging flower baskets, I was not sure what I would face on my short-term experience. I prayed for courage, wisdom, and patience, for I desperately needed God by my side.

We stayed at a lovely hotel facing the Atlantic Ocean. The prospect of teaching somewhat familiar women within my church at their annual retreat was daunting. I had heard of their uneasiness regarding my topic. Though the beach venue was serene, the natives were restless.

After I described our craft of pictures on poster board, I sensed a ripple of resistance among the group of women. I prayed for the Holy Spirit to calm all of our nerves and instill a bit of childlike whimsy into the air. A bit of humor would help, too, I added to my fervent prayer.

Besides the teaching I had prepared and the Bible I gripped for support, I took weapons of scissors, glue, and paper to disperse among the wary women.

I could practically see the walls grow taller and thicker when I pointed to the instruments and explained the craft, which included cutting pictures out of magazines. The blank stares warned me I had spoken a foreign language.

As soon as I mentioned the word "Godography," I could tell I had pushed the boundaries and lost the trust of my natives. Perhaps their culture was offended by my vernacular. I quickly assured them the word was not obscure fantasy nor ancient mythology. While it could not be found in the dictionary, the definition of "Godography," creatively connected, did have merit. To regain trust, I first had to confess that I, myself, had invented the word—it was not a trick.

"Godography," I explained, "is God's biography, or story, in you."

Everyone's life is a journey with a unique and special story unfolding along the way. Real life is a provocative story and can be envisioned as a horizontal line. Yet, in every story, every life, there is an intervention from God. He intervenes in our lives, bringing salvation, redemption, and eternity, much like a straight vertical line piercing through our life center. With confidence, we can visualize our own lives in the shape of the cross.

When God intercedes, real-life stories become stories of truth, His truth.

Our stories are God's stories—His testimonies. Finding God in the process of reporting, writing, drawing, or symbolizing the details of your life, is a way of retrieving the essence of your life. Godography.

Many of us live our days on the surface with …what we have, what we are doing, where we are going, and who we are serving, helping, and/or teaching. We speculate, plan, and create. Instead of following God, we look toward the result, the investment, or the consequence, and we lose the life of *now*.

I suggested if each lady were willing to pick up scissors and glue and embark on the craft of looking for God in their lives, they would end up with a portrait of the true essence of their lives—God's grace. By creating a collage of personally unique pictures, words, and phrases, they would discover their stories.

What unfolded in the ballroom of our hotel was nothing short of miraculous. As the women flipped through magazines, snipped scissors, and ripped out pictures and words, God clearly brought life and light into the room. From every worktable, memories were lifted, renewed, and recreated. The women laughed, chatted, shared, and cried as the individual pictures they found created the tapestries of their lives.

As they abandoned their fears, expectations, and pretenses, the retreat ladies became my missionary women and began teaching me as they shared stories of real faith lived out in the battlefield of life. I, too, shed my anxiety and caution. We all became transparent as pictures, sayings, quotes, verses, and songs revealed God's grace in every collage; His intervention was evident in each story. Broken were shackles of abusive pasts, shady relatives, misguided morals, bitter relationships, broken dreams, and failed promises to God. The golden thread of God's saving grace highlighted life on each poster so that every collage was a personal portrait of redemption and joy.

How the tears flowed when the retreat came to an end and we, all sisters in Christ, embraced each other as friends forever. The walls had been shattered and the weapons recreated into ties binding our lives together. The mission trip was a success.

When we surrender ourselves to our Creator and look for Him in our lives, the details of our past become God's glory today. No matter where we go to find Him, He will "make all things new," and He will be exalted!

"Then you will call upon me and pray to me when you seek me with all your heart. I will be found by you," declares the Lord. (Jeremiah 29:12–14)

CONFESSIONS OF A FLUFF BALL

I was ten when we had just returned from shoe shopping and I helped search the neighborhood for my little brother who had a penchant for escape. Mom, Dad, and friends called out his name, scouring front and back yards. We had to be careful because the sidewalk was roped off where new concrete had just been laid. It was me who first saw our escapist trudging behind a garage, and me who went running after him as fast as I could.

"There he is! I FOUND him!" Oh, how proud of me they all would be! But the more I ran, the faster my brother went and the heavier my brand-new red shoes felt.

"STOP!" was what my parents were yelling, not "Hooray!" In my dramatic show of heroism, I had immersed my shoes in a winding lane of wet concrete.

"You are a Fluff Ball" was my mother's comment as she tossed the red shoes, heavy as bowling balls, into the trash.

I am a Fluff Ball. My mother told me so, over and over again as I flitted and twirled through my youth with my heart on my sleeve and my head in the sand. I am idealistic, whimsical, guileless, and prone to speaking in metaphors, dancing in the kitchen, and having crushes on men who look like Jesus. I can drive Rule Makers crazy—ice cream for breakfast, dinner invites to strangers, donuts for workmen.

Once I figured out Jesus is more interested in my heart than my practicality, it was easy—a relief actually—to hand Him the mess of me.

Then I discovered He had rules of His own. He wanted me to be holy.

> As obedient children, do not be conformed to the passions
> of your former ignorance, but as He who called you is holy,
> you also be holy in all your conduct . . . (1 Peter 1:14–15)

Peter, the disciple who could have been my distant cousin in the Fluff family, was the deliverer of this non-negotiable mandate. "In all your conduct," he wrote. How is it possible to rise from the muck of failure to divine virtue? Peter's story gives me new perspective. Impetuous, passionate, and unreliable, Peter wrote about the process of becoming holy because he, too, had to drop his junk in Jesus' lap.

Peter, Simon at the time, was desperate for approval. Maybe he had been the older brother living up to expectations of responsibility to set the example for his siblings. He adored Jesus and tried desperately to prove his worth by chasing Him on water, grabbing soap from His hand to wash His feet, and agreeing with Him through gritted teeth to forgive sinners seventy times seven.

Approval is a deadly and illusive ambition for a Fluff Ball. Driven like Peter, I aspired to gain my parent's approval. I was the oldest of four, but my brother, a brilliant man (who resembles Jesus, by the way) was my mother's favorite and is probably to this day, though she is no longer living. Our family was no more dysfunctional than most in the 50s and 60s. Without therapy, a gym, or Oprah, my mother fought her demons with alcohol, prescription drugs, and temper tantrums. After long, nighttime parties my parents had with neighbors, I washed glasses, scrubbed chip and dip bowls, and threw out limp, soggy leftovers. I kept everything in order while dreams danced in my head. Academically mediocre, I strived to excel in good behavior. It would have been easier to be smart!

I could think of Fluff Ball as an endearment, but the title remains a stigma I've tried to slough off for too many years. I need a new nametag.

Peter got one, eventually. The ink was drying on the paper when Jesus saw the fisherman throw down his life's work, a fish net, to hang with the Man who said, "Follow Me."

I did not check my kids into daycare permanently when I followed Jesus, but I quickly enrolled them in Sunday school, signed up for a beginner's Bible study, joined a church, and much to my husband's chagrin, put our five-pound Bible smack in the middle of the coffee table—open. I might as well have hung a banner on the front of the house, "Jesus lives here!"

"Fluff Ball" was just one of the names my mother and husband mumbled about me then, barely under their breath.

Years later, after my father died, my mother finally fought off her terrors. But she still called me Fluff Ball, even though I took care of her when she was sick, had grown children of my own, and could place my husband's Bible next to mine on the table.

Peter's compulsiveness turned to shame when he ran to hide from his enemies. In fear of losing his own life, he denied knowing his beloved Friend. What he had not known was that his old life was already gone. Jesus had given him a new role and a new name. Peter was still trying to live up to Simon's expectations when he realized the travesty of trying to be what he could not be. He finally surrendered to all that he was meant to be.

In his true identity, the one Jesus had given him, Peter became bold, courageous, and filled with the Holy Spirit.

And I tell you, you are Peter, and on this rock I will build my church, and the gates of hell shall not prevail against it. (Matthew 16:18)

What could Jesus do with a Fluff Ball?

Release her from the shackles of approval and crown her with Love. Bless her with a husband who tells her she is beautiful and guide her with three daughters who call her wise. Shower her with ten rollicking grandchildren who call her fun, hilarious, cool, and a "Present Lady." Allow a crippling disease to enter her life just enough to keep her humble and aware of the preciousness of mobility. Give her worship music to dance to in the kitchen and turn her extravagant faith into a craft that exclaims to the world with all the imagery and metaphors of a Fluff Ball, He has come to set us free from the past to the joy of His holiness in the present.

Thank You, Jesus!

Therefore if anyone is in Christ, he is a new creation.
The old has passed away; behold, the new has come. (2 Corinthians 5:17)

STAR

Many are called, but few are chosen. (Matthew 22:14)

For many, becoming a Christian is like suddenly becoming a star on stage. One minute, we are lost, struggling, confused nobodies feeling like zeros, and the next instant, we are filled with joy, confidence, and purpose. We "put on the new self, created after the likeness of God in true righteousness and holiness" (Ephesians 4:24). Rather than "stardom," it could be "Crossdom," when the Light of our Savior floods our souls, and we dance out on center stage, filled to the fingertips with His love! The Lord, the producer of this Christ-assured ecstasy, plans it this way so that we experience the fullness of our salvation before we go out into the world and practice our new life in Him. Although the story is His and the plot has been written, the practice gets tougher from venue to venue, and sometimes, it seems the bright lights of salvation waver.

At the age of three, I became a Star. I know this to be true because the proof of it is preserved in three faded 5x7 photographs I found tucked in a tattered photo album in my mother's attic.

I don't recall what my role had been on that makeshift wooden stage; perhaps a somersault or toe-tapping jingles. I was obviously thrilled with myself. The first photograph showed me beaming, not at the camera, but my discovery of stardom. Not with humility, but with glee, I bowed. That was depicted in the other two pictures; evidently, I bowed again and again. Basking in the charmed adoration of my spectators, I bent my round torso, threw my head to my scraped knees, and bowed as I'm sure my teacher had taught me to do. Bottom up, arms flung past the flowered tutu, tumbled piped pigtails brushing the platform . . . I reveled in my audience's favor.

Somewhere between ages three and seven, I lost the glory and power of being a celebrity, much like what happens to us when we lose the "heavenly vision" of our calling and our ardor for evangelism. We step off the stage of salvation glory and become weary with the task of practicing faith. Leaving behind the inspiration of Holy Spirit applause, we work hard at the vision that we have re-scripted, only to find it illusive.

This sad spiritual disillusionment reminds me of another opportunity at stardom I had when I was in the second grade. I was to simply walk on stage with a glass half filled with milk and recite the line, "Don't cry over spilled milk." I was then to exit the stage. Not much time for a budding Star. For some reason, though, I had a really hard time with my line. I just could not remember the words, and there was so much pressure! My teacher told me to quit fidgeting and speak louder, my mother made me stand in the middle of our hallway to practice over and over, and the sentence played games in my head. The problem was, *I didn't get it.*

Every time I spilled milk at the dinner table, it was a disaster. My mother jumped up, grabbed my plate, yanked my napkin, and sopped up the mess while my father launched into his "Pay Attention" lecture. Spilled milk ruined meals at my house, and I cried every time. How could I stand in the middle of a stage and declare in a loud voice, "Don't cry over spilled milk?" Didn't everyone?

A Christian must be true to the vision given by God, not to somebody else's idea or to an adapted similarity that seems comfortable and easier to perform and more popular. God's vision is real-life action, not the world's program.

I was not able to perform my role at the school assembly. In front of everybody, I began my recitation, "Don't cry . . .," and I suddenly froze, center stage. In nervous hysteria, I laughed uncontrollably. My teacher had to come from behind the curtain to escort me, doubled over with insane giggles, backstage. End of performance.

I was not disobedient to the heavenly vision. (Acts 26:19)

When God chooses His beloved to participate in His eternal plan, He wants only for us to know the full magnitude of His love. We are to bask in His love—sing, dance, and rejoice in it and bow down to His glory. Just like the three-year-old ballerina had twirled in her stardom, we are to celebrate our "Crossdom."

To be true to the "heavenly vision," as Paul had been, we must remember the Director of our lives selected our roles, and we are perfect fits. We will not be left confused, confounded, or in the dark to chase after that which we don't understand. We will gain confidence in our faith as we learn God's truths from His Word. We can trust God to lead us into that which we are to become in His Kingdom, His stage in His story.

God's vision for us, the "heavenly vision," is to be who we are every day, doing what we do every minute, to please Him by obeying His Will as He reveals it to us, and to walk in our faith as He guides us.

Practicing the Gospel in daily life is serious business. It will take God all of eternity to make us conform to His purpose. When we perform for God only, His Son will be the bright star shining through us. No acting experience necessary!

"Therefore, brothers, be all the more diligent to confirm your calling and election, for if you practice these qualities, you will never fall." (2 Peter 1:10)

GET SMART WITH JESUS

I remember two things about sixth grade—Mrs. Cheek, my math teacher, and Janice Horton. Word problems were my nemeses, and Mrs. Cheek was the teacher who demanded solutions, not stories. I struggled to get the grade my father expected of me, but that *C* was on shaky ground. How I envied Janice Horton, the girl with long brown hair who could play kickball as well as the boys, got straight *As*, and made Mrs. Cheek smile. Mrs. Cheek didn't smile often. Despite her high heels, spoofed black hair, and red lipstick, the woman was all numbers and no slack. She had no imagination; and students like me drove her crazy. At times, I saw her staring at me through all that mascara, trying to figure me out. Dad gave me the same look years later when he tried to teach me how to balance a checkbook.

The numbers in the word problems often made no sense to me because I worried about the farmer who sold so many dozens of apples. Would there still be apple pies, and how did they peel those apples anyway? Janice kept the numbers in straight columns. Her binder had tabs filled with papers decorated with bright red *As* on the top right corners of the pages, above her name.

When Janice and I became friends, I could not believe my good fortune. To this day, I don't know what she liked about me; perhaps, I was her comic relief. Being with her made me feel smarter, so I tried to be more like her. My mother bought separators for my binder, and I pretended to like math. I did my homework, spent extra time on the problems, and kept my notebook in order. The grades on my quizzes hovered at a *C*, even a *C+*. I desperately wanted Mrs. Cheek to think I was smart like Janice, but, despite all my hard work, I knew failure was just around the corner.

Just before the end of the school year, Janice, a child of a military family like me, moved away, leaving me without my best friend and any hope for success in Mrs. Cheek's class. The day of final tests arrived, and I was on my own. Trying to focus on numbers and solutions rather than people and problems, I barely completed the test before the bell rang.

Days later, walking down the rows in her black high heels and red pencil skirt, Mrs. Cheek returned each student's test paper, folded vertically, on their desks. When she put mine in front of me, she smiled. On the top right corner of my unfolded test, above my name, was a red *B*.

"You are smarter than you think," she said, her eyes locking on mine. Her heels clicked on to the next desk. Dumbfounded, I felt a power released within me. I was smart! I'd just have to work hard sometimes, particularly with numbers.

Seeking God can feel like trying to be smart or figuring the solution to a math problem when you are a writer. Most times, it's easier to serve God than to be still and wait on Him.

There are amazing and inspiring Christians around us who do things for God. They build churches, travel on mission trips, run soup kitchens, teach Sunday school, preach at the pulpit, sing in the choir, and lead worship, all while raising families, holding down jobs, and balancing the onslaught of daily living. When we try to do as others do for God's Kingdom and can't keep up, we feel like failures. We look at what other folks accomplish and give ourselves a poor grade. We don't seek God. As I had tried to be like Janice in the sixth grade, we often try to be like we think God wants us to be. Instead of receiving His peace, we lament our lack of peace because we can't find Him. So we try harder.

Jesus went to His Father continuously; He *needed* God so that He could do what God wanted Him to do.

We, too, need God for what He calls us to do. We need His presence to guide us, His peace to reassure us, and His power to enable us. But we can't always get away to a quiet place to be with God. The world yanks at our intentions and life exhausts our energies. How do we seek God when we can't find the way?

Jesus gave us His perfect example and left us with His power.

It is the Spirit who gives life; the flesh is no help at all.
The words I have spoken to you are spirit and life. (John 6:63)

While Jesus ministered on the earth, He was able to pull away from the crowds and find quiet places. He did not have another job, carpool, children, or a cellphone, but He had multitudes of people surrounding Him. Over and over, He turned from them and looked to God.

In His wisdom and compassion, Jesus gave us the power to receive His peace whenever we choose to turn our minds to Him, no matter where we are or what our circumstances. When we choose to look at Him rather than our situation or the accomplishment of others, we receive His peace as He promised.

Peace I leave with you, my peace I give to you. Not as the world gives do I give to you. Let not your hearts be troubled, neither let them be afraid. (John 14:27)

When we worry our way to God, we block our ability to walk freely with Him and, ultimately, to be effective for Him.

We don't have to work our way to God; He is within us. He knows we are smarter than we think!

BAT WOMAN SAVED

A bat flapping in a tree, that's what I was before I asked Jesus into my life. Blinded by the enemy of self, immature and myopic, a mother of two under four, my husband deployed for months at a time, I was exhausted, lonely, and disillusioned. Family life on "Father Knows Best" had never given me a hint of life behind the scenes. I'd dreamed of being like Margaret Anderson with fresh lipstick and my apron on when Jim came in smiling for dinner. Instead, I found myself amid wailing babies, messy dogs, and bell-bottoms that were too snug.

I'd wanted a happy family, picnics, strolls in the park, bike rides, flowers under the window, a cocker spaniel, and my husband home at five, preferably smiling. God would protect if needed, though it had never occurred to me He would be close enough for a relationship. I hoped He could handle my greatest fears—death, storms, and my babysitter cancelling on me.

When my girlfriend invited me to Bible study at her church, I was reluctant to accept, until she added, "free childcare." The following Wednesday, with blankies, pacifiers, and bottles in tow, my little ones and I were ready to go. This is how Jesus first cracked open the door to my heart and shed a glimmer of light on my bat wings.

I felt like a nocturnal beast exposed in a sunny field of flowers. All those lovely women with long curly hair, welcoming embraces, and quilt-covered Bibles gave me the jitters. They didn't know about my bad habits or how I yelled at my kids.

The only Bible I owned was a tabletop *Readers Digest* King James, which was on the closet shelf so it wouldn't be used as a coloring book.

I continued to attend the Bible study, however, and not just because the childcare was free. I was being taught about the love of Jesus, and I saw how peaceful it looked on the faces of the women who greeted me every week. Theirs was a "beauty of a gentle and quiet spirit." (1 Peter 3:4)

Their joy was real, even though like me, many of them were mothers of small children, who managed homes with laundry and pets, and had husbands away on deployments or who worked late into the night. Beside their friendships with each other and the Bibles they carried like purses, the ladies appeared to have something stronger on their side, a hovering bodyguard. You just wouldn't want to cop an attitude with any of them. I watched, listened, and learned.

Even the ladies who didn't know me made me feel welcome. Sometimes, they appeared thankful when I arrived and gave me an extra wide smile or a pat on the shoulder. I began to relax during the weekly discussions and listen to the prayers they shared.

Let no corrupt talk come out of your mouths, but only such as is good for building up, as fits the occasion, that it may impart grace to those who hear. (Ephesians 4:29)

I struggled with my identity in God's creation and could not perceive evidence of grace like theirs in my life, only faults and temper tantrums. Like Zacchaeus the tax collector, I felt hated and despised. How could God ever love me?

When I was brave enough to admit my fear and bold enough to ask for prayer, my new friends beseeched God on my behalf, not about my character flaws but my real need. Little did I know at that time, they were acting through the Holy Spirit, just as Jesus had with the blind man and tax collector in Jericho. I needed salvation.

For God so loved the world that He gave His only Son, that whoever believes in Him should not perish but have eternal life. (John3:16)

"Jesus died for my sins." I heard this over and over again but could not con-nect with it. If He had died for me, what did He want me to do for Him? Stop yelling? Quit smoking? Go to Africa? What if I couldn't be good enough? Would I be asked politely to stop attending Bible study?

The faith I had was just not working.

Finally, I knelt by my bed, as I had seen them do when I watched "Little House on the Prairie," with my kids, and like the blind man, I begged for mercy, quietly so I wouldn't wake them.

"Our Father Who art in heaven," was all I knew. I felt I needed to start with formality. "Please will you help me?"

"Jesus, I give everything to You—my children, my husband, my dogs, my thighs, and all my fears. If You'll have me, I give You my life and You can be Lord of my heart. No surprise to You, but I am a sinner, and I am asking for forgive-ness. Amen." My prayer was rudimentary.

I confess I expected something magical to occur—a rainbow in the night sky, a phone call from my husband at sea, the Cat in the Hat to clean my house. Nothing happened. I got up from my knees and climbed into bed where I slept soundly until morning. The days continued to tumble along, my husband sailed in and out of town, the girls were fussy, the dogs messy, my temper flared occa-sionally, and the Cat never showed up. But there seemed to be an invisible guard at every turn, and the peace I felt was unmistakable. Praying became a conversa-tion between Jesus and me as I relinquished my fears. My Bible study developed into daily lessons, the girls and I attended church, and I prayed that one day, our family would worship together. I wanted Jesus in our home.

I didn't realize it then, but Jesus had heard my prayer *loud and clear*. He had stopped in His tracks as if Bartimaeus, the blind man, was crying again for the Son of David; turning the universe to get to the Book of Life, He called out my name and wrote it down.

Today salvation has come to this house . . . (Luke 19:9)

Thanks to the faith, love, and prayers of those who went to the women's Bible study for Jesus and not childcare, I am no longer a baleful bat. Fifty years later, I am still loved by the Son of God. Our home is full of Jesus, gloriously alive in my husband, our children, grandchildren, family, and friends!

And immediately he recovered his sight, and followed Him, glorifying God. And all the people, when they saw it, gave praise to God. (Luke 18:43)

THE PLACES YOU WILL GO!

As I consider God's plan for my life's journey, I defer to the rollicking imagination of Dr. Seuss. After all, I am skipping along in my seventh decade and might benefit from a bit of literary humor.

- "Try something different, try something new! You might find it likes you and you like it, too!"
- "If you have brains in your head, you have feet in your shoes you can steer yourself any direction you choose!"
- "Whatever you do, do it well, do it *you*!"

Though the clever cat knew how to have fun, his advice didn't guarantee easy street or dreams coming true. One can get very turned around and confused following his or her feet with every whim or choosing a path that's just right for *me*.

God's vision for His followers takes them on a straight path that always progresses toward a goal—His goal. It is tempting to follow the vision rather than keeping in stride with God and letting Him lead us along the way, especially if there is an unexpected change. When a detour blocks our vision, the journey can be painful and frightening. We are apt to forget to trust God.

My friend, Barb McCarty, and I took a road trip from Frankfurt, Germany to Pisa, Italy fifty years ago. This jaunt was not as glamorous as it sounds because our three little girls, all under age four, accompanied us. Before deploying from the States, my husband had purchased a small Mercedes Benz. The plan was for me to pick up the new car in Frankfort and use it for travel in Europe while he was stationed on a Naval aircraft carrier in the Mediterranean Sea during the Vietnam War.

Barb's and my goal was to drive to an Army base near Pisa and set up temporary housekeeping until our husbands' ship ported in Naples, only three hours away. Since many of our friends' husbands were also serving on carriers, but flying missions off Vietnam, we felt invincible—our husbands were reachable within a relatively close and safe arena.

Our vision was to be united with our husbands, pure and simple. Otherwise, two twenty-three-year-old women driving nearly six hundred miles through three foreign countries in a shiny new stick-shift sedan with three babies stuffed in the back seat while following a map for guidance on foreign roads, was ludicrous. Foolhardy we may have been, but our objective overcame our fear and common sense. At that time, I was not personally following the Lord, but He was fast on my heels. As I look back on it, I see even then, I was being taught the concept of faith.

Just three hours into our trip, we hit a snag. The signs along the roadway, which coordinated with the line on the map we were following, suddenly changed. We could see the road on the map, which would take us to Strasburg and Switzerland, but the sign in front of us read, "*die Umlietung.*" We had taken no turns off our road nor followed any other signs. But we were definitely on "*die Umlietung.*" Neither of us spoke German, so efforts we made to stop by roadside markets and fuel stations to ask for directions were fruitless. Cell phone and Google were not yet vocabulary words in the early 1970s.

We decided to follow "*die Umlietung*" hoping it was leading south; we knew if we ran into a body of water, we were in big trouble. The hours passed as the miles disappeared and dusk settled in. Our only comfort was the knowledge that we had not deviated from our strange new road.

The three cramped passengers, dope-eyed and full to their ears with stale pretzels and animal crackers, wailed and flailed in various stages of meltdowns. Any sense of ease we felt in the rising chaos plummeted when the road before us ended at a gravel pit with wooden barriers and the same sign: *die Umleitung.* Feeling as if we had been transferred to another planet, I stopped the car and stared ahead at the rocky field.

Barb pointed to the tattered map she had been clutching for hours. "There's no field, park, or mountain named '*Umleitung*' anywhere! Who knows where we are?" In the days of no cell phones or GPS, smoke signals were our best bet. Barb lit a cigarette.

I felt panic scratch an adult-sized meltdown of my own just as I noticed a signpost by a road not far from the field. I turned the car in its direction and recognized the lettering on the sign to be the same road on our map that we had started on almost a full day earlier! By nightfall, we found ourselves back in line with our map and tucked into a quaint *gasthaus* for the night.

The traumatic trip made sense days later, when, with our husbands' help, we were able to translate *die Umleitung* to "Detour." All along, we had been following detour signs. We hoped in what we could not see on our map and kept driving.

Years later, when I read Hebrews 11:1, "Faith is having confidence in what we hope for and assurance about what we cannot see," I realized I had actually persevered in faith when Barb and I followed that German detour sign. God knew then what I would learn about Him later!

Detours, like change, are rarely factored into our life journeys, but they should be expected with God. When they block our way, along with other potholes, traffic, and mountains, we must persevere through those troubles and strive to stay in stride with Him. We can be like Enoch, who "walked with God" (Genesis 3:24) until he was *with* God.

God's detours strengthen our faith, teach us obedience, and increase our trust in His Word. As David wrote, He is "a lamp to my feet and a light to my path." (Psalm 119:105)

And, "Oh! The places you will go!" (Dr. Seuss)

And the Lord went before them by day in a pillar of cloud to lead them
along the way, and by night in a pillar of fire to give them light,
that they might travel by day and night. (Exodus 13:21)

YOU'VE GOT MAIL

People who read other people's mail have a problem. They betray the trust of both the letter writer and the recipient just to get information—private information. I used to be just such a person. I was desperate to know if the letter I was compelled to open, though it was not addressed to me, contained any thoughts about me. People who open other people's mail are also insecure, maybe even lost.

The letters I wanted to read were the ones my father sent to my mother while his ship was deployed during the escalating conflict in Vietnam. I was a sophomore in college and had decided to change my major from education to humanities. My parents possibly thought I'd be a better teacher than a thinker, so they recommended I come home to reevaluate my future. I left my friends, freedom, and fresh ideas to live in a townhouse with my mom, two brothers, and baby sister. My mother found a job for me at a bank (a poor fit for an aspiring thinker), and I floundered around, having no idea what I was going to do with myself forever.

Many of the letters Dad had written were piled neatly on my mother's dresser, so I could conveniently replace them in order after I had read them. I scanned the letters with aching hunger, trying to find my name somewhere in my father's familiar scrawl. I felt so ashamed of what I was doing, but I couldn't stop. Did my dad still love me? Had I failed him by leaving college? What did he expect of me now? If only he would send a letter addressed to me.

Mom was so busy with the other kids and involved with the Navy wives who were also coping with separations and horrifying news of young pilots being shot down, killed, or lost in Vietnam that she hardly noticed me moping around or sleuthing in her bedroom. She had her own battles and had no interest in dealing with an emotional exile, one who cried over chipped nail polish. So I clawed through her letters to find my place.

Isn't that what we do with the Bible sometimes? Looking for solace, encouragement, and love, we scan the Scriptures for something familiar, something to grasp, and something that clearly says our name. Sometimes, it can be frustrating when reading the New Testament. Paul, Peter, Timothy, and the other Apostles wrote letters addressed to people, villages, and churches miles and generations away from our needs today. What did they know about broken water heaters, computer crashes, or the outrageous cost of Disney World Fast Passes? How can we read those letters and still feel included and understood? Can the early church's mail teach us how to experience grace and peace with family members, neighbors, and strangers? Yes, it would seem that if the Epistles had been addressed to us personally, they would be more relevant:

Greetings Meredith!

The Lord would rather you not call other drivers "jerks." He didn't give you grace and peace for nothing, you know.

Fortunately, the Bible is the inspired Word of God, not a compilation of random letters. A friend who was a wise devotional writer pointed out, "This is one of the most marvelous mysteries of our faith, that the Word of God is the living Christ." All that is written in the Bible was not just written for the people of the times. Through the Holy Spirit, the Word of God is alive in anyone with Christ in his or her heart.

Heaven and earth will pass away, but my words will not pass away.
(Matthew 24:35)

Peter, in his letter addressed not to us but to "God's elect, strangers in the world, scattered throughout Pontus, Galatia, Cappadocia, Asia and Bithynia . . ." reassured them that even though they had not personally been with Jesus as he had, they were heirs of all His promises.

> Though you do not now see Him you believe in Him and rejoice . . .
> obtaining the outcome of your faith, the salvation of your souls.
> (1 Peter 1:8–9)

This is our assurance also. The letters from the Apostles may have been addressed to other people, but because of our faith, the messages were intended for us as well.

When I read my father's letters, my name was rarely in the lines. But his words of encouragement to my mother, his accounts of adventures in foreign ports, and his promises of fun and happiness when he returned included me in his words. The letters may have been written to her, but I was woven into his thoughts of home and family.

The Old Testament was directed specifically to the Israelites, God's Chosen People, and is about why God called them out of Egypt, led them to a Promised Land, and how He expected them to live.

> Therefore you shall keep His statutes and His commandments
> which I command you today, that it may go well with you,
> and with your children after you. (Deuteronomy 4:40)

Intertwined throughout the promises and instructions to the Israelites was a greater promise to all of mankind. God would send a Savior through whom anyone could be adopted into the family of God and receive all of the riches of His kingdom, including grace and peace in abundance.

> The Spirit himself bears witness with our spirit that we are children of
> God, and if children then heirs with Christ. (Romans 8:16–17a)

The letters of the New Testament with all of their wisdom, encouragement, and promises were written for believers in Jesus Christ, "God's elect." Unlike me, covertly searching my father's letters for reassurance, we can—and must—openly read the Letters of the Apostles because they were written with our names all over them.

Yes, you've got mail!

SMELL THE BACON

The sense of joy and freedom God pours upon a new Christian is intoxicating. Some forty years later and settled down by God's grace and long-suffering patience, I now know the gay abandonment I felt after Christ took over my heart and soul was exactly what I had needed to solidify my new life in Him. However, it was not quite what my family and friends, who did not know the same joy, had needed or necessarily liked. My faith needed filtering.

It wasn't long before I prayed to go to Africa, or somewhere, to be an evangelist, teach the Bible, serve the church, and go with Jesus to "Feed my sheep!" I wanted to get out of town.

Like the man whose gazillion demons were drowned in a sea of pigs, I thought if I went away with the Lord, my past would be forgotten, and I would sin no more. Sure, I was a little over-zealous and unabashedly emotional about anything Jesus, but I had no problem with that. At least, like the formerly demonized man, I was no longer a "dead (wo)man walking." I was alive, well, and could move mountains if needed.

Unfortunately, the people in my family were used to moving their own mountains and keeping things under control their way. I, who used to cower and sulk, was now suddenly cheery and sing-songy. It was maddening to them.

"Stop singing that song!" my mother finally blurted out one day as I belted out Fred Hammond's lyrics to "This is the Day the Lord Has Made" for the hundredth time to my little girls who were just as happy and frolicky as I was. My feelings were not hurt one bit. I hummed.

"Go home to your people," Jesus told the man who had wanted to flee the town of his past and get on a boat with his Savior. I, too, was sent to go back to normal and focus on home and family, where Jesus had met me in the first place.

Trying to be a Christian my way, I had become an extravagant evangelist, bringing Jesus into every gathering, conversation, and argument. I joined Bible studies, led summer Bible camps, started my own Bible study, and even taught Christian aerobics. I soon became an exhausted evangelist.

"Come to Me," Jesus asks. I was definitely an embarrassed evangelist when I realized I had been trying to be Jesus rather than be with Him.

We are most effective for the Lord when our lives reflect what He has done for us, not by our preaching or teaching. For many, the hardest place to live out our faith is in our home with our families or in our neighborhood with our friends. Even though Christ through salvation has forgiven us, sin, like oinking pigs refusing to be drowned, plague us:

"Oink"—fear.

"Oink"—doubt.

"Oink, oink"—pride.

Until Jesus calls us to a mission of His choice rather than ours, He wants us to spend time at His feet. We do this by drawing near to Him in prayer, reading His Word, and listening to His voice within us. It is the only way to get rid of those pigs.

. . . and they came to Jesus and found the man from whom the demons had gone, sitting at the feet of Jesus, clothed, and in his right mind. (Luke 8:35b)

What a picture of serenity! The wretched man, whose life had been terrorized by demons, was now relaxing and chatting with Jesus.

". . . and they were afraid." Sure the townspeople were afraid of their maniacal neighbor who had emerged from the tombs with familiar features but was now a vastly different man.

"Will they trust me?" Perhaps the once-possessed man wondered if he would be welcomed there when Jesus had told him to go back home. Maybe he had a wife and children who would run away from him. Nevertheless, with gratitude for his new life, the man got up and went back to his town and showed the people what the Lord had done by treating them with the love and forgiveness Jesus had given him. If he had any more encounters with demon-pigs, Jesus Christ just fried them. They smoldered like burnt bacon as the man became a powerful evangelist, not only in his hometown but in its outlying cities as well.

Once I took off my Jesus suit and relaxed into my faith, members of my family and members of their families eventually found their joy in Christ. Several of our friends then gave their lives to Him also.

Many of these people have had amazing ministries, gone on mission trips (even to Africa!), and become powerful teachers of God's Word. At times, I have worried about how imperfect or ineffective I have been in the Kingdom of God (*Oink! Oink!*), then I remember the faith-filled lives of my family and friends and am reminded that Jesus is in charge of the Great Commission, not me.

We are cleansed from the inside out and created new when we give our lives to Christ. As we lean into Him, He changes us right where we are, preparing us for His unique call on our lives. At times, we may feel like we are in the frying pan, but we are really in the process of being set free from our pigs, His way.

PRESSING IN PRAYER

Now there was leaning on Jesus' bosom one of His disciples,
whom Jesus loved. (John 13:23)

, too, want to crawl into Jesus's lap. This is how I want to pray:

"Lord, as I recline against you, hold me tight. Please keep me from becoming distanced, distracted, downhearted, and disenchanted. If my eyes droop, my shoulders sag, or I lean over to sneak a peek behind You, jolt me to my soul. Grab my attention quickly and pull my face to Yours. Press me against Your chest so hard that I feel Your heart pounding. Let me not loathe Your Love but desire it above my days. I want to remain so close to You that my eyes are riveted on Yours, and the warmth of Your breath permeates my flesh. What can come from Your Heart that will help me this day to do Your will?"

If only I could be spiritually correct and pray like inspired biblical writers. Instead, I go from prayer-perfect to prayer-personal.

"Lord, if I could stay in this place at least until lunch, we would have a happier time of it. The dogs are barking, my husband is rustling his paper—hinting for breakfast—and there's an exercise class I really wish I could attend. I need to go, but I didn't get my whole prayer in; I haven't reminded you about the kids, the finances, the president, or my back . . .

Well, You know about the pain in my back. I think even the mailman knows about my back. You must be rolling Your eyes over my litany, 'WHERE ARE YOU . . . I GIVE UP—HELP! Help. Help. Help. HELP!' I do not understand why I get no relief from these spasms. Is there holiness in pain, some kind of nobility? I just don't think I can hold out as long as Job did, and I thank you very much, but I don't really want to be blessed twice as much for my patience. Twenty grand-children would cause crowd-crises in our converted family room.

Paul certainly suffered spasms of his own kind. His struggle with that thorn is almost palpable in Scripture, yet You said to him, 'My grace is sufficient for you, for my strength is made perfect in weakness' (2 Corinthians 12:9). Does that mean when I am weak in Your weakness, I am strength-perfect? Maybe my pain has more to do with living the power of the Cross than it does with dying to be healed. I'm with Paul on that one—I want to 'know Him crucified!' Is this grace, Lord? Please tell me it is.

"I still don't know how to pray effectively and correctly for the nation and our crazy mixed-up government. Do I need to be politically correct? All I know is our country seems to be going south, and I don't know how to help. Remember Peter after the Holy Spirit came rushing in like a reality commercial? He was bold, passionate, and unplugged. He could rally a crowd and set them straight! 'Men of Judea and all who dwell in Jerusalem, let this be known to you and heed my words' (Acts 2:14). Whoa! Bring it on!"

Who would ever have thought the bumbling bravado disciple would become a great orator? There's no mistaking the fire of the Spirit in Peter's words.

"I want that Fire, God. I want to be upside down crazy about all of Your ways, doing cartwheels for You, which would be pretty miraculous at my age.

By the way, what about that guy at the seafood counter? In spite of his withered hand, he slings that shrimp around and wraps the tuna while laughing and carrying on with the customers. Remember when he waved at me from the store's second-story cafeteria as I crossed the parking lot? He made my day! God bless him! Really bless him.

And then there is Lin, the manicurist with the limp and bowed back. She can't be more than four feet tall. I didn't think she spoke English until I learned differently when I asked if she had children (I felt Your nudge, thanks). In her sweet melodic English, she told me she has two children she raised alone. Her son received a letter of congratulations for scholastic achievement from President Obama, her daughter wants her ears pierced but she's only seven, and all three of them recite passages from the King James Bible together. 'Some time I don' understan' many words. But Truth is easy to see.' Lin smiled. That's a lot of wisdom packed into four feet!

Lately, my daughters and friends have been writing down their thanks for big and little things, pasting the notes on walls and refrigerators, or saving them in jars. Thanks to Ann Voskamp, there is an attitude of gratitude spreading from one town to the next, sort of like a safety net beneath the fiscal cliff. The numbers of graces counted are rising higher than the national debt. Maybe our politicians should consider a thanks tax rather than tax tricks. It is miraculous, this Gratitude Game.

Forgive me, Lord, for not being diligent enough to keep a ledger of thanks. Most of the time, I'm just too flabbergasted about Your blessings to write them down, like when I found that parking place right across from the computer store, just after I'd whispered a desperate little prayer because my back hurt and my briefcase was heavy. I pulled my car into that space and shook my head, 'Wow! Thank You! I'll have to remember to write this down.' And I never did.

Lord, I feel better now. Your lap is so comfortable. Thank You for Your company. I hope I didn't talk too much. I was desperate when I came to You a little while ago, in pain and so lonely. You heard my cry and lifted me up. This must be the answer—first grief, then grace, and then gratitude. Is it possible for wisdom to come out of whining? Hmmm. We'll have to talk about that later.

Time to let the dog out and fix breakfast. Amen!"

May we always go to God. Though it may not be a perfect prayer, it is our personal prayer. He is our Father and He listens.

I waited patiently for the Lord, He inclined to me and heard my cry.
He lifted me out of the miry bog, He set my feet upon a rock
making my steps secure. (Psalm 40:1-2)

WHAT WILL YOU WEAR?

There is a loose photograph, slipped between the back pages of our wedding album, developed in color, a special treat for the photography of the 1960s. My husband, in a brown sports jacket, is leaning down toward me. With my hand on my wide-brimmed navy blue felt hat, my head is tilted upward to receive his kiss. I am dressed in a cobalt blue suit with three-quarter-length sleeves and a pencil skirt.

My husband was a Navy fighter pilot and a well-known prankster among his squadron mates, most of whom were either in or attending our wedding. Dan's most recent mischief had been a ploy he masterminded to kidnap the bride of the unsuspecting groom and escort her to an all-night bowling alley. The nocturnal bowling caper was thwarted either for lack of comrade support or a leak of confidentiality, but the prank was not forgotten.

To say that our groomsmen and their buddies had a score to settle with my new husband was playground talk. These men, trained to drop bombs and kill people, had a vendetta. I was a wanted bride.

I almost did not get to wear my coveted blue suit and wide-brimmed hat, which I had purchased with all of my savings and kept on lay-away for months. My plan, my dream, had been to wear it on my wedding day when I made my debut as "Mrs. Daniel Bunting."

The black and white photograph that did make it into the plastic-covered pages of the wedding album is the hallmark of a bride and grooms' first dance.

My hand in his and his arm curved around my waist, we gazed dreamily into each other's eyes, or so it seemed. In reality, my husband and I were having our first argument. Having gotten wind of a scheme brewing among the avenging wedding party, Dan knew our quick escape was imperative. He suggested I pretend to leave for the powder room and meet him where our car would be waiting.

"There is no time for farewells. Your suitcase will be in the car." I saw no tenderness in his eyes, rather a glint of steel.

I could not fathom leaving my wedding without a grand farewell exit with me dressed in my smashing cobalt suit and a wide-brimmed hat. I looked up at my husband of one hour and refused. The photographer snapped his camera.

I narrowly escaped my all-night bowling spree, thanks to the quick-acting and cunning maneuvers of family members, and I did say my farewells dressed in blue. I held onto my hat as my frantic husband whispered down to me, "Go!" Someone took the picture.

It seems important to dress appropriately for an occasion. We want to fit in and make an impact, a statement, or perhaps create a stir. Women apply make-up and men put on a tie, all to look their best on the outside. Just as I, the bride, had donned my suit and hat to be a wife ready to enter the world with my husband, we all put on the outfit that describes our purpose: teacher, speaker, CEO, librarian, or socialite. We are masters of covering up who we are on the inside.

> Though He had done so many signs before them,
> they still did not believe in Him. (John 12:37)

After giving exhaustive testimony and proof of His deity to His people, Jesus Christ came to the end of His ministry, and turning to the Gentiles, He embarked on the path to His crucifixion.

Even though the Jewish rejection of Jesus as the Messiah was predicted in Scripture so that God's sovereign plan to rescue all people would unfold, Jesus the Son of Man was troubled.

Now my soul is troubled. And what shall I say?
"Father save me from this hour?" But for this purpose, I have
come to this hour. Father, glorify your name. (John 12:27–28)

Jesus knew His time on earth was short, but before He suffered rejection, denial, and agony, He wanted to impart the essence of His purpose on earth to His beloved disciples. So He gathered them for dinner and washed their feet.

At this point, Jesus' identity was pretty clear to the twelve men whom He had mentored for three years. Peter knew He was the Christ (Matthew 16:16), and he and his friends had given up all of their livelihoods to sit at the feet of their Master. Jesus was their Messiah, their King, and their Savior. To give them their last lesson, Jesus could have worn majestic robes embedded with gold, silver, and jewels. Yet even such indescribable finery would not have adequately framed His glory. In His humility, Jesus proved His holiness.

Jesus Christ, King of all kings, "laid aside His outer garments, and taking a towel, He tied it around His waist" (John 13:3). He then picked up a washcloth and basin and proceeded to wash the crusted, calloused feet of each one of His disciples, even those of Judas Iscariot, who would give Him over to His killers. Jesus' outfit was not what the world around Him would have expected. He made His impact by wearing a servant's cloth. His lesson was this: "I have given you an example that you also should do as I have done to you" (13:15).

As I write this, we are approaching Thanksgiving and Christmas, with all of its gathering, gorging, commercialism, and materialism. I wonder: can we remember the simple elegance of our Savior and the example He told us to follow? Can we shake off the world's expectations and demands, unbutton our stress, unzip frustrations, pull off our rush, toss our lists, release our anxieties and inhale—love? Can we honor Christ by first giving thanks for one another and then simply by serving others? We need only to be dressed in His Love.

By this all people will know that you are my disciples,
if you have love for one another. (John 13:35)

GRACE IN THE DEEP

When Jonah opted for a cruise instead of obeying God's command to go to Nineveh, he found himself at the depths of the sea, and in the belly of a fish. The story of the obstinate prophet is comical on one hand and arresting on the other. You may remember the great fish of the sea large enough to ingest a whole man and can imagine the horror of being encased in the gurgling, smelly gut of a sea monster (Jonah 1–2). What we can't imagine, until we read about Jonah, is at what lengths God will go to give grace—all the way to the bottom of the sea and farther.

Ultimately, at the end of all his resources, Jonah has an epiphany, changes his attitude, and prays. In spite of his fear, distress, and misery, Jonah acknowledges that God is with him and hears his cries. With thanksgiving, he promises to sacrifice what he wants in order to do what God wants.

> "And the LORD spoke to the fish,
> and it vomited Jonah out upon dry land." (Jonah 2:10)

Undeserving, disobedient, rebellious Jonah was drenched in messy redeeming grace. He was saved from the sea to bring God's word to a lost people.

I love this short story because it celebrates God's relentless grace, not only to a pouting prophet but also to a land of naughty people.

Tim Keller wrote, "No human being is so good they don't need grace, or so bad they won't be given grace."

Lately, I've been wondering where the grace is for the good person. Where is the saving, merciful, peaceful grace for the haggard man standing on the street corner with a cardboard sign, the family whose child was killed by a drunk driver, and, closer to home, my friend in the last drawn-out stages of cancer while his wife of merely five years, still trusting Jesus, holds his hand and gives him water with a Q-tip? If God is bountiful in grace and offers it abundantly to those who have chosen to turn from Him, where is His grace in the pain and suffering for innocent, righteous, and devoted Believers?

Paul may have thrown these same questions, albeit with more eloquence, to the Giver of Grace when he was afflicted with a debilitating physical, emotional, or abusive problem that kept him from becoming more effective in his call to bring the Gospel to the Gentiles (2 Corinthians 12: 9–10). He must have been frustrated and disappointed, maybe devastated at first, when he imagined his whole ministry falling apart. Where was God's grace when this fully chosen, sacrificial, righteous man-of-God was stopped in his tracks by a thorn?

I can relate to how Paul may have felt. I once had a ministry focused on faith and fitness in which my physical stamina and strength played a big part. Since I was older than most fitness instructors at the time and had once been fairly sedentary and overweight, my empathy and energy resonated with many people suffering from lists of poor habits and lost hopes. My encouragement to have faith in the plan God made for each one of us to be "be well and in good health, as it goes well with your soul" (3 John 1:2) restored new hope and healthy lifestyles for many clients.

When rheumatoid arthritis made its painful way into my joints, I was rendered miserable and immobile most of the time. I had to leave behind my active lifestyle and fitness ministry, and I railed at God the whole way. It just did not make sense. My mantra "Movement is life" seemed to be a cruel joke. Where was the grace in this?

God had words with Paul, and I am so grateful for them. He basically told the ailing Apostle to stop complaining and get on with his work. It was just that Paul's work was going to be different now, bathed in God's grace.

My grace is sufficient for you, my power is made perfect in weakness.
(2 Corinthians 12:9)

Paul's affliction became his strength because he had to depend on God to continue his ministry. Now, because of his reliance on God and gratitude for the ability given to him to continue to address the churches of Europe, his passionate messages were real, humble, and empathetic. Jesus Christ from the cross was given the glory, not Paul's appointment, credentials, or eloquence.

After decades of pain, surgeries, and deformities, I, too, learned to trust God's plan. The reliance I once had on my image as a fitness guru changed to humble gratitude for just being able to move. My mantra took on a more important truth, one that I could share from experience: movement is what God gave us to live abundantly in His Kingdom, no matter how fit we are. Whereat first, I despaired my disabling disease, God poured grace on my hardened heart, giving me a fresh message to share and a supernatural joy that even helps me laugh at my crooked hands.

Until we really get grace, we cannot live the life God, in His sovereignty, has chosen for us. Yet, His grace comes in different ways than we expect and usually comes when we are underwater, feeling like a fish has swallowed us. The life and work God calls us to are always much different than our plans, dreams, or visions. Many times it carries us through hardship, suffering, pain, even grief—the refining sacrifices Jesus made at the cross so that we would know we are never alone in our afflictions.

With God's grace, Paul said, "Therefore I will boast the more gladly of my weaknesses, so that the power of Christ may rest on me." (2 Corinthians 12:9)

So, this is grace: the power of Christ resting upon us during our greatest need. We don't have to strive in our weakness to be stronger, calmer, or better. Grace calls us to rest in Christ as He gives us the power to face what had before seemed impossible.

"Salvation belongs to the Lord" (Jonah 2:9). This is how Jonah closes his prayer, just before he is lifted from the sea.

The choices are God's, and the reasons are His alone. The grace He gives is sufficient for the rebellious and especially the righteous. His undeserved favor is enough—the perfect amount of kindness going beyond what is deserved. This grace is the power of Christ resting on us to cover our weaknesses, keeping us secure and at peace with Him. Grace pulls us from great seas of doubt and despair to a place of trust in the goodness of our Sovereign God.

THE BEST IS YET TO COME

The moment I saw my father the last time he visited me, I had a sense of his history having been written. My first taste of grief was bittersweet. As I welcomed him to our home, my heart whispered, "Goodbye."

Dad's eyes twinkled and his white hair billowed from under his U.S. Navy ball cap. He looked oddly frail but trim and tanned beneath his worn freckles. Although he had been a red-head as a child, I only remember his hair being black and how magical it had seemed that he could grow a beard of orange and brown.

He wore his favorite ball cap, as he always had since the days he served on the U.S.S. America. As a Naval officer of twenty-six years, his last tour aboard the new aircraft carrier had been the glory of his career. Traveling distant waterways on the glistening ship while serving his country, my father entertained military officers and dignitaries in the ship's cabin and wined and dined with diplomats and celebrities from all over the world. For the consummate host, it was the best time of his life.

Just a year after that visit with us in Virginia, I traveled to my parents' home in Florida to be with my father before he died. By then, the cancer that had been nesting within his body was flourishing savagely. The new foundation of faith upon which I had been standing rumbled beneath me. Life is a series of goodbyes, I decided—a very sad thought indeed.

The Lord is my shepherd, I shall not want.
He makes me lie down in green pastures.
He leads me beside still waters, He restores my soul.
He leads me in paths of righteousness
for His name's sake.

I walked closely with the Lord in those days, skipping actually, as a new Christian in love with a fresh lease on life. It was hard to demonstrate my faith and not give in to my emotions when my mother called me to my father's bedside. By then, my husband had retired from the Navy and was immersed in a new career. I went to my parent's home alone where my mother, in her own suffering, turned her back on my prayers and tears.

Even though I walk
through the valley
of the shadow of death,
I will fear no evil,
For You are with me:
Your rod and Your staff,
they comfort me.

I held my dying father's hand, trying to will my flesh and blood into his bony grip. Words remained garbled in his head as his ice-blue eyes, filmed and weary, stared at my face until love took over and his chin trembled. Amazingly, his hair was still a full white crown.

As a child, I first learned of God's love through the wise words and strong faith of Gramma Rene, my father's mother. But Dad had always remained private about his relationship with God. Like the centurion in Luke 7, he was a man of honor and charity but maintained a proper distance from confession. Believing my faith was enough to save his life, I prayed with him at his bedside through the long nights, telling him of God's mercy and eternal peace.

I was with him for six days, trying to will him back to health. Six days of praying, coercing, and begging God to wait, reconsider, redeem the time, and take the opportunity for a miracle. I read my Bible, searched for a reason, a hint to the secret that would cure my father. Beneath my anguish was desperation to know God's sovereignty in what my faith could not grasp. What would become of the man who had been my rock all of my life? How would I go on without him? God's silence was deafening.

> You prepare a table before me
> in the presence of my enemies;
> You anoint my head with oil;
> my cup overflows.

Dad suffered fitful days and sleepless nights during my visit, but Sunday, the day I had to fly home, dawned bright and beautiful—a day of promise. By mid-morning, the hospice nurse had him washed, dressed, and sitting comfortably in his wheelchair. His smiling face had a fresh shave, and his U.S. Navy ball cap topped his neatly combed hair. The color had returned to his skin, the film was gone from his eyes, and his body seemed sturdy and sure. He even had a twinkle in his eye when I asked if he wanted to go for a walk! The nurse agreed that fresh air would do him good since he was responding so well to his medicine. Full of hope and renewed faith, I wheeled my father out the front door.

We walked down the sidewalk to the pathway overlooking the gulf where the boats and small ships sailed into the harbor. Dad's words still got stuck in his head, but he didn't seem to mind, and we both enjoyed our one-way conversation. The sparkling water beckoned us closer as my father, once again the venerable sea captain, scanned the ocean with a practiced eye. I know now the Holy Spirit whispered, and I took up the cue.

"Just imagine!" I ventured. "Out there, coming toward us, that great carrier, your ship—the U.S.S. America!" I believed so hard with him that for a split second, I thought I saw a gray form with the unmistakable mast of an aircraft carrier hovering on the horizon. "And *you* are here to salute her!"

My father beamed as he said with certainty, "Yes, and the best is yet to come!"

Those words were the ones I shared with our family and friends as we gathered together at my father's memorial service ten days later. God had surely answered my prayers and had given my father peace. They are the same words that have comforted me over the years whenever I've been tempted to question God's ways and decisions. Grief is the heaviest burden, but God promises us that with Him, life is not about the "goodbye;" it is all about the "hello again."

Surely goodness and mercy shall follow me
all the days of my life.
And I shall dwell in the house of the Lord forever. (Psalm 23)

EVANGELIST CRYING

Being an Evangelist can be tough, even agonizing work. I speak from experience. You have to dump everything: your dreams, expectations, pride, and heart. Sometimes you have to cry in front of everybody. Then you let Jesus pick up what's left of you to use for His purpose and His alone.

I was an evangelist of sorts, once. My relationship with Christ was still new and in the throes of oblivion. I simply adored the One who had set me free and wanted to serve Him in any way He asked. Washing and ironing clothes for three peer-pressured girls was not my idea of serving in the Kingdom. Nor was making four breakfasts, four lunches, and planning meals for five exactly what I thought the Lord had in mind. Driving from school to school, making beds, and chasing three dogs? No, this was not the mission field to which I deserved to be assigned; of this I was certain.

> He said to Him, "Yes Lord, you know that I love You."
> He said to him, "Feed my lambs." (John 21:15)

Just two months before Easter, the call came from Claudia, our adult Sunday School class leader. Claudia was a businesswoman who dressed in tailored grey suits, low black heels, and wore her hair in a tight bun. She seemed to me a very disciplined individual, void of much emotion. Every so often, I would catch her peering at me through her glasses.

Over the phone, Claudia told me that in preparation for Easter, our group would be studying Jesus' last days on earth.

"We would like you to teach the six-week study." Her voice was monotone. Was she joking? Were they looking for a childcare superintendent during the session? I would have accepted that request, though not wholeheartedly.

Claudia was serious: "We'd like you to teach the class. It's just six weeks."

This woman had not heard that as a Kindergartner, I had been pulled off the stage wailing or that I had flunked speech class in my senior year of high school.

What was she thinking? What was *God* thinking?

My first thought was "No!" but I asked the Sunday School leader what she wanted me to teach. *What exactly is the topic?*

"Jesus."

"I'll do it." Who would turn down Jesus? Either I would fail or Jesus would come through for me.

> And because of Him you are in Christ Jesus
> who became to us wisdom from God. (1 Cor. 1:30)

Immediately, I began studying. I read through every Bible translation I owned, researched concordances, borrowed books, memorized Scripture, and prayed while I made lunches, sorted laundry, and ran the vacuum cleaner. By the time I was ready to teach the Sunday School class about Jesus, the Savior and I were BFFs, best friends forever.

> For consider your calling . . . not many of you are wise
> according to worldly standards . . . (1 Cor. 1:26)

"We've got this," I told Him. I didn't tell Him about my nerves, the ones choking me. I figured He knew already. Burgeoning with facts and burning with passion, I stood before twenty or so adults in our class, including friends, my husband, and Claudia. After a quick prayer and a deep breath, I opened my mouth . . . and started to cry. Horrified by my behavior, I gulped back a sob, only to have the tears start over again. I could not talk; every word brought on a fresh onslaught of emotion. I stood there in my tear-stained mess, frozen until Claudia led me outside the room to the water fountain.

"Are you all right?" You don't have to go back in there, you know," she suggested.

I found my voice. Or more like God's voice found me. "If I don't try again, I'll never be able to go back." With mascara-smeared and swollen eyes, I walked into the classroom, apologized, and taught my first lesson.

I wish I could report that the following lessons were easier for me, but they were not. Though the attendees and I never suffered through another meltdown, I continued to be jittery, emotional, and entirely dependent on the mercy of Jesus. I felt like a failure in my mission field and was humbled that at least I hadn't been fired. I was relieved when Easter arrived, and my only responsibilities were to go home to fill baskets and cook a ham. In His wise way, God had shown me the richness of my tasks.

Years later, as I stood in line at a bagel shop, the gentleman in front of me turned and asked if I was "Meredith."

How did he know my name and who was he?

"You probably don't recognize me," he said with a smile, "but I'll never forget you. My wife and I were new in the area when we attended the church where you taught a Sunday School class about Jesus."

Oh, dear.

"You cried," he continued, "but we were so impressed that in spite of your anxiety, your passion about Jesus kept you with us and you stuck it out. So we joined the church, and now my wife and I are serving there as its youth leaders."

I stood there, bagel bag in hand, tears streaming down my face—again.

As Christians, we all want to serve Jesus as best we can—even better than we can. He called us to "feed my sheep," so we try to prepare gourmet meals and travel the earth with riches from America. If it so happens our Lord deems it necessary for us to evangelize, we strive to do it with eloquence: No crying allowed. We must remember, though, it is not our success He wants, only our willingness to go and serve where and when He calls us.

I am the voice of one crying out in the wilderness. (John 1:23)

Literally.

WOW FACTOR

If you are a lover of a gooey mix of chocolate, caramel, and peanuts, you've probably bitten into a Snickers bar a few times and have been delighted by those promised peanuts "in every slice." It's a jaunt out on a limb to compare those peanuts to the act of worship, but the similarities can be imagined.

For Christians, worship is the nugget within our gratitude for the enduring character of God: His love, goodness, and faithfulness. When we experience God's grace through the forgiveness of our sins, redemptive freedom from those sins, and the promise of a life in His care until we are united with Him, we are blown away by such amazing love! Our gratitude is expressed through praises, songs, and shouts. Like the peanuts in the candy bar, worship is solid, rich, and a little unyielding until crunched when it explodes with savory saltiness. The people of God are exhorted to come into God's presence all pea-nutty—jumping, clapping, and singing with joy!

I am not a candy lover, except for when it's a Snickers bar filled with chocolate, caramel, gooey magic, and crunchy peanuts—the best!

Recently, I discovered Snickers has outdone itself by being filled with peanut butter, rather than just peanuts. The peanuts nestled in the magic pudding are mixed and mashed into one nutty chew, bite after bite, with no crunch to interrupt the burst of flavors. Wow!

I want to worship God with the same lung-filling, eye-opening, lip-smacking, "Wow!" I felt when I bit into my first square peanut butter Snickers bar. The wow factor is wonder and praise combined, with no number, category, or rules to confine it. It is all at once an explosion of brain chemicals and pinging senses at the instance of intervention with the miraculous. It has no sound other than deep breathing and heart pounding for gratitude to the Giver from the undeserving recipient. God gives us all good things.

I wouldn't be surprised if the sad, used-up woman, who trudged to the well when she hoped there would be no one there to recognize her, said "Wow!" under her breath when she met the One who really knew her. Possibly Zacchaeus thought, "Wow! Jesus coming to MY house for dinner?" And how about all those kids Jesus gathered into His lap in spite of all the grown-ups' grumbling? Wow! Surely, exclamations of "Wow! Wow! WOW!" in Aramaic, trilled along the mountainside where hundreds of weary travelers were fed a banquet of fish and bread after the Teacher had given them the secrets to the Kingdom of God.

Wonder is a "Wow!" with a thank you at the end of the exhale. A flight overlooking the Grand Canyon, a rainbow flung above a parking lot, the birth of a healthy baby, a spot that's only a mole, an improved lab report, Handel's Messiah, or the appearance of a radiant Star in the east—they all cause chills, wonderment, and awe.

When I behold the grace of God's intervention in my life, "Wow!" is the all-inclusive word of the moment. It is then that I want to hug a stranger, pay for a policeman's coffee, and make blueberry pound cake for ambulance drivers. Worship from a heart of gratitude naturally makes the praise giver want to serve. God's gifts evoke such a filling that it overflows in love and goodwill. We serve with gladness.

Tears also often follow wonder. This is why some of us cry when we "enter His gates with thanksgiving and His courts with praise" (Psalm 100:4)! Worship evokes emotion as we open ourselves to the surrender of all-inclusive gratitude, even for the things we didn't expect and don't like so much. Like the peanuts in the old Snickers bars, our worship is pulverized by the power of the Holy Spirit, and our praises create a revival of a renewed faith.

Not only can we experience the joys of God's presence in our everyday lives, but we can rest on the promise of His steadfast love forever. Better yet, we are assured that our descendants are included also in His holy membership.

The Lord, the Lord, a God merciful and gracious, slow to anger, and abounding in steadfast love and faithfulness, keeping steadfast love for thousands, forgiving iniquity, transgression, and sin . . . (Exodus 34:6)

Wow!

GOD'S TEARS

Taking no creature comforts to Honduras, not even makeup, our daughter, Leslie, packed capris, tank tops, flip-flops, and three cans of bug spray into her duffel bag. She then filled her empty suitcase with bubbles, stickers, crayons, paper, Frisbees, T-shirts, underwear, socks, and small books about Jesus. Ones just the right size for little hands.

Praying she would not contract malaria, succumb to motion sickness, or get bitten by a poisonous bug, Leslie joined her mission team and flew to Honduras to spend ten days helping at an orphanage. These were her words:

"As we drove through Honduras, the second poorest country in the Western Hemisphere, my heart was shattered. It is commonplace to find children foraging for food among piles of trash, families in tarp-covered shacks the size of my minivan, people burning plastic inside their homes to eliminate any bugs carrying malaria or dengue fever. It's not right how these people live. The kids at the orphanage seem to be the lucky ones."

Leslie carries her heart in her hand where it is exposed, and she cries. She still cries like she did when she was three, high-pitched, gulping sobs with pools of tears streaming down her cheeks as she blows her agony into tissue after tissue.

This is the child who went to the mission field and came back as an evangelist. Leslie, a mom who pours adoration on her three children, could not contain the love she has in her heart for other children in the world, a love some won't ever receive from parents like her. So she went to Honduras to find them.

A missionary, whether experienced or not, must serve with a heart completely committed to Christ, for the work can be hard and heartbreaking. It is a challenge and a sacrifice to work in a foreign country with a different culture, food, language, and religion, and labor in extreme conditions where insects and rodents abound. For my daughter on her first missionary trip, the most difficult adjustment was seeing the lost, broken, desperate people—children especially—and not being able to *fix* their plight.

After exhilarating and exhausting days at the orphanage, Leslie sent emails to family and friends all over America.

"I want to put a little six-year-old boy in my suitcase! I want him to be in our family, laughing, learning, and sleeping in his own bed, in his own home."

Ninety children had been rescued from wasted, oppressed, and abusive conditions and were being fed, educated, and given medical care at the orphanage. Here, Leslie and her missionary team rolled up their sleeves to give the worn-out staff a hand and, more importantly, bring Jesus where He was needed.

In love and tenderness, the Lord was there with them as they played games, read stories, sang songs, wrestled, and hugged those love-hungry kids. Then, He drew close as the missionaries rocked and consoled lost babies, whispering, "Jesus loves you, this I know" into tiny ears under matted hair, and wiped away paths of tears.

Somewhere in Honduras, not far from the orphanage, there is a young woman sleeping in a shack, walking the streets, or possibly foraging cast-off tins for food. She has an abusive husband and no children, at least not now. A month ago, she had five children: Esther, Luis, Johanna, Lorraine, and Naomi.

This impoverished, abused, and hopeless mother brought her five children to the orphanage and gave them up. In horror, Leslie watched the woman sign the paperwork, unwrap the clinging arms of her baby, and walk away.

Later, rocking the bedraggled, bereft baby, the same age as her own daughter at home, Leslie had to hold back her sobs so as not to disturb the sleeping child.

"I sometimes wonder why such lost souls must be dependent upon the charity of those God has called. Why won't He just rescue them?" Leslie emailed from her cell phone.

There are some who are called to serve in the Kingdom of God and others who are served by the Kingdom of God. If those who are found did not rescue those who are lost, God's love would never be shared. Even the forgotten little ones further His Kingdom because their plight calls the missionaries, laden with the Word of God to their side, and their hearts get filled with the love of God, and they, in turn, share His love with others. This is how a village is saved, one by one, sharing the Gospel.

The entire missionary team knew about the mother of five and prayed to God for mercy and provision. Then they took her story and their prayers home to their families, friends, and churches. Within a few weeks, that mother was raised to the heights of Heaven by thousands of prayers, while her children were nourished with food, care, and the love of God. The needs of the orphanage were spread and met by those who were touched by that woman's sacrifice. With her last desperate act of maternal love, the Kingdom of God rose!

One Sunday, Leslie spoke to her church's congregation about her trip to Honduras and the children who still own a piece of her heart. Before she was to speak, she texted me to pray that she would not cry.

"How can I talk about those kids and *not* cry?" she typed.

As I prayed for my daughter, God whispered, "Let her cry. Those are My tears."

OUR GREATER HOPE

I am writing from my chair at the Infusion Center where the medicine that keeps the inflammation from searing through my joints is being pumped through a needle into my veins. While I hope the medicine will give me relief from debilitating pain, I have three hours to reflect on a greater hope.

The hope that gives peace in the darkest hour is the same gift given to us when we want to feel better, need a break from a toilsome day, or are tired of the rain. It is a call to consider the work of Christ in the Kingdom of God. When life in the present seems too chaotic, painful, or mundane, we beseech God for action. We hope for what we want. I hope for something or other every day:

"I hope I can find my keys."

"I hope I won't be late for my appointment."

"I hope the medicine works."

Those were some of my hopes so far today. Simply put, I hope God has got my back. I am tired of being sick, slow, and surly. I am at the end of myself.

Hope is a natural go-to in misery, despair, and fear, but often, we slip into the wrong hope. As I did today, we hope for the things that will take away the pain. We pray for a better day, something new, or someone to understand us. We do not pray as David did.

Let the morning bring me word of your unfailing love, for I have put my trust in you. Show me the way I should go, for to you I entrust my life.
(Psalm 143:8, NIV)

David's hope was ensconced in God Himself and the love that he knew would not fail him. Rather than asking for sunnier weather, a clear plan of attack, or protection in battle, David wanted only God's love to remain with him. Hope is not a whim of despair; it is the weapon that destroys it.

The Lord is my strength and my shield; my heart trusts in Him, and He helps me. My heart leaps for joy, and with my song I will praise Him.
(Psalm 28:7, NIV)

Wallowing in self-pity wishing for anything that will help make our situation improve is not the hope God has given us. As Christians, we are not to hope for what we want from God: we are to hope for Him alone. Until our trust is in God, our hope is despondent, despairing, or even desperate. We are not seeking God; we are begging Him to do something.

When I am preparing dinner, and my swollen crooked fingers cannot operate the can opener or open up a zip-lock bag, I am often unhappy about needing help for so many minor tasks. Do I rejoice in the hope of eternal life, the place where my whole body will be in perfect shape? No, I hope my husband will take me out for dinner. When he doesn't but instead opens the can for me, I am thankful he is there and always willing to help. This is the higher hope God gives to us—being able to see our blessings, not our failings, and being grateful even in difficulty.

In Luke's Gospel, there is an account of a widow coming to Jesus with her only son who had just died. Her despair is palpable on the page of my Bible: "And when the Lord saw her, He had compassion on her and said, 'Do not weep.'" Can you feel the love Jesus had for this woman who lost the only one in the world who could care for her? In her despair, she went to Jesus.

And He said, "Young man I say to you, arise."
And the dead man sat up and began to speak. (Luke 7:14, NIV)

When we feel we have lost everything we care about and we despair in our hopelessness, the grace of God pours His hope into us. It is He who catches us before we fall. It is He "who has loved us and given us everlasting consolation and good hope by grace" (2 Thessalonians 2:16). This is the saving hope that gives us an inexpressible sense of peace and comfort. In His everlasting arms, we will be given all we ever need.

Years ago, my husband and I were desperate for our daughter's return from the British Virgin Islands where she just had fallen off a cliff while on her honeymoon. We prayed fervently for her safety and strength as she was strapped to a bodyboard and airlifted back to the States. Meanwhile, the plane she was on went through a wicked storm, tossing the small prop all over the sky. If we had known about that imminent danger, our prayers of desperation would have turned to panicked pleas. Desperate hope blinds us from the power of our Almighty God.

After her safe return, our daughter told us, "I wasn't afraid because my hope was in God who had created the storm in the first place!" Her hope was not desperate but fixed on God's glory.

Martha was very distraught while she waited for Jesus to come after her brother, Lazarus, had died. We can just imagine her anguish when He finally arrived as she said, "Lord, if you had been here, my brother would not have died." Yet in her grief, she still had abiding hope.

> I know that whatever you ask from God,
> God will give you. (John 11:21–22, NIV)

This was the glorious hope to which Jesus responded, "I am the resurrection and life. Whoever believes in me, though he die, shall he live."

The hope that God gives us is poured into us by grace through the Holy Spirit and reminds us that we are saved. This promise is sealed in the resurrection of Jesus Christ and extends beyond any fix, big or small, we are in. It is our only hope: to be in glory with Christ eternally.

May the God of hope fill you with all joy and peace. (Romans 15:13, NIV)

A LIGHT IN THE PIT

Recently, I asked the Lord for a closer relationship with Him and, as a special favor, perhaps some new wisdom. I have found Him to have a sense of humor, as He has kept company with me through my grandchildren. And He has taught me a few lessons along the way.

Taking a break from the swimming pool on a warm summer day, my two grandsons got Vernors ginger ale from the fridge and sat down in chairs on the deck to play a game of Monopoly. The oldest grandson, almost ten, was proud and possessive of the deluxe Monopoly game he had received for Christmas, and he set it up with meticulous care on the table in front of us. The breeze was blowing a bit, frustrating him when some of the paper bills fluttered out of place. He was furious, though, when his younger brother grabbed the floating bills and placed them either upside down or in the wrong slot of the money rack. That Hunter, the seven-year-old, wanted to be Banker was entirely out of the question. The game belonged to Childers; he was the oldest and every piece of the Monopoly set was to be kept in order and perfect condition— not a responsibility worthy of a seven-year-old, evidently. The bright afternoon started to get cloudy.

The picturesque game on the deck with my grandsons required calming, consoling, and finally, conciliatory action. I would be the Banker, keep all the money straight, and yes, each boy could have a popsicle. As they glared at each other, licking and slurping their frozen sugar, I thanked God for whoever had invented popsicles. Surely, she was a mom of the past who knew how to bring just a few moments of peace to summer vacations.

For a while, the game progressed without incident, each boy moving their metal pieces around the board, passing GO!, collecting two hundred dollars, and buying up property as fast as I could collect their bills and dole out change. Childers, who named himself proprietor of the property, kept the cards neatly in color-coded order and watched me like a hawk to be sure I, too, kept my bank straight. Hunter, meanwhile, with orange goo smeared down his chin, eyed the pool. The game was losing his interest fast, and the tension spiking from his older brother was painful. Soon, either the game or a boy was going to end up in the water. We needed a diversion; another popsicle was not an option. I prayed silently for wisdom and a solution.

When I accidentally dropped my newly acquired, "Atlantic Avenue" card on the floor of the deck, I could feel the air around us get sucked in. As the card flipped over on the floor, then slipped down through the plank and under the deck, all three of us froze. This was not the diversion I had been looking for.

"Oh no. Oh no!" Childers whispered hoarsely. He looked at me in shock, the freckles on his face, usually a sweet blur of amber, became blotches of red on his whitened skin. If I had been his brother, he would have attacked me. As his grandmother, I knew I was safe from assault. But the panic and heartbreak I saw in my grandson's face over the lost card were worse than any berating I could have received.

Atlantic Avenue, lying in the dark dank ground beneath the deck, was beyond our reach. I prayed for wisdom, thinking, "I know how that card feels."

"There's a door!" (With Jesus, there is always a door!) I assured Childers, whose eyes were swimming with tears. "There is a door to climb through to get beneath the deck so the card can be found!" I tried to sound confident as visions of mud, spiders, roaches, and maybe a rat or two under the deck made me shudder. What if he asked me to go under there and find the card?

"We'll never find it under there. It's too dark." Childers's voice was hollow.

Hunter's face lit up bright, "I know! We'll use a flashlight! Somebody can go under there with a flashlight and find it. It's not lost forever!"

The seven-year-old's wisdom spoke to the depths of my soul. Unless buried, anything can be found with the right light, even a city under a deck, or those who feel they, too, are lost.

This story with its simple plot became a profound epiphany for me as the week progressed. It was a difficult week with the loss of our beloved dog, my sporadic back spasms kicking up again, and a general, yet familiar, malaise settling over me like a woolen shawl. I had been praying for a better mood, a little energy, and basically, for Jesus to take over. Like the card under the deck, I felt lost in the pit I had fallen into.

When I remembered the Atlantic Avenue card in the dirt and how the bright light from the flashlight led us to it, I realized there was also a light shining on me: the Light of the world. I wasn't lost; I am always found because that bright, glorious Light is within me. I could loll around in the muck all I wanted, but as soon as I chose to tap into Christ, I would rise and flourish in the life given to me by God.

Since then, I have had the sense of a new "on" switch, stuck to my heart with a holy ability to feel the glorious light coming from it. Despite grief, pain, and fatigue, the Light of Christ is eternally switched to *on*. Not only can I see my way through some dark days, but I also know His Light is shining outward. Once again, God has poured His grace over me, His Light lifting me into His Presence.

Motto: When playing games with grandchildren, be sure to carry a flashlight.

Truth:

... let your light shine before others [and grandchildren] that they may see your good works, and glorify your Father who is in heaven. (Matthew 5:16)

LOOK FOR HIS GATE

What gate do you like to go through to spend time with the Lord? Where do you go to search for an answer, make a decision, change your mood, ask for forgiveness, or reflect on the day? Where do you go to inhale the Holy Spirit and exhale grace?

Some people take their Quiet Time while running. I remember long runs with the Lord when I didn't want to turn back. Other seekers go to a chair or a room or grab sunscreen and head to the beach. Gardeners find quiet solace with worms and bulbs in the Creator's dirt. Heaven only knows where mothers of small children can find a nook of peace. We all need time alone with the One who loves our soul, the One who calls us to be with Him.

I think my mother thought she found God when she went shopping. Whenever she pulled up to a store or mall and found a parking place right in front she would exclaim with satisfaction, "There must be something in here the Lord wants me to have!" In she would go, looking for Him in her own way, as happy as if she had a ticket to heaven in her pocketbook!

When I wash dishes, I gaze out of the window above my sink, leaving food particles on silverware and pots. It's embarrassing. I have no idea what my hands are doing in the soapy water. The important part is my thoughts of Jesus.

The arbor and gate at the back of the yard have my attention, not the dishes. Our backyard is alive with memories. It has been the scene of engagement celebrations, dozens of Easter egg hunts, thousands of barbequed hamburgers, decorations for every season's holiday, many birthday festivities, Fourth of July and Labor Day hoopla, swimming instructions for ten grandchildren and three dogs, a graduation party, and more golden pink sunsets melting beyond the fence than can be counted. This yard has embraced our family, and our lives have evolved within. But I keep gazing past the back gate at another world.

Beyond the gate lies a pristine golf course with cropped Bermuda grass, rolling hills, winding cart paths, and trees along the fairways. Even when the course is being played by groups of four, mostly riding in golf carts, the voices traveling in the breeze are hushed, almost reverent. In every season, there is a signature beauty along the paths of eighteen holes spawning seven miles of faithfully tended nature.

Sometimes, if it is not in play, I can walk the golf course. Usually, I can only look at it wistfully, knowing its peace. It possesses a Canaan-like quality, a spiritual pull. I must go and be there. I leave my world behind and step forward with purpose.

Stepping forward through the gate for a walk on the golf course begins my time with Jesus.

We all want perfect serene places to be intimate with our Lord. We want to hear Him call our name. The meadow, the seashore, or mountaintops are idyllic pastures to be with the Shepherd who promises to tend to our every need. Where is the gate through which we can go and close out the cacophony of our daily lives? It doesn't always lead to a golf course.

Having recently returned from a seven-week vacation in Florida, traveling in a motorhome with my husband, I discovered that Jesus is the gatekeeper of extraordinary vistas in the form of stories. While our RV has many comforts of home, such as a dinette, a bath and a half, and a standard-sized refrigerator, we are still confined to the area above the wheels! Dan is a clever, intelligent, and articulate man who processes his many interesting thoughts out loud. Though we enjoyed each other's company and the fun we had, space and silence were not easy to come by while we were on vacation.

I prayed for a way to give God a greater measure of myself over the weeks of Lent during our time away from home but was frustrated with my worship. It seemed I was either crowded or interrupted.

In the recesses of my soul, God opened His gate. He showed me that quiet and space are not requirements for His Presence. The people I met were to be my place of worship. They held the gates through which I would find Christ. Dog walkers, campground neighbors, bartenders, shopkeepers, and strangers along the sidewalks—they all became the places I could surrender myself to Jesus. Just with a smile and a greeting, I was blessed in return with stories shared, joys imparted, and the gift of new friendships. The gates of Heaven flew open, and I celebrated Lent on vacation!

> I am the gate. Whoever enters through Me will be saved.
> They will come in and go and out, and find pasture. (John 10:9, NIV)

Going in and out the Jesus Gate, wherever it leads—to fairways, stores, or people—must be intentional. When we want Jesus, *need* Him for refreshment, recovery, restoration, or rejuvenation, we must go to His gate and walk through it fully expecting to find Him there.

He is there, you will discover, because He has always been with you and always will be with you. His Presence will fill you when you go to Him and boldly ask Him to meet you at the gate.

There, Jesus, your shepherd, welcomes you.

> The gatekeeper opens the gate for him, and the sheep listen to his voice.
> He calls his own sheep by name and leads them out. (John 10:3, NIV)

WE ARE ONE

Hanging on the wall of our kitchen above years of meals, cooking, dirty dishes, seasonal dishware, dog bowls, food commentary, and a million family conversations, is a weathered blue wooden sign that reads, "Family is everything." That sign has seen it all: the spilled milk, emotional outbursts, warm hugs, grateful kisses, newborns suckling, grandparents gazing, couples nuzzling, homecomings, birthdays, graduations, laughter, and tears. Within the kitchen walls is the spirit of our family, from crises to ceremonies.

When my husband and I married fifty-plus years ago, we both left our respective families and joined together to be our own new family. We didn't change our personalities, jobs, interests, or several of our irritating habits, but we committed to love one another. Our standards, principles, and goals became one, and we worked (sometimes very hard) to establish and live by them. Over the years, we multiplied and became a large family. It was when we made a commitment to Jesus Christ, experienced the power of the Holy Spirit, that our personalities changed. Our family became God's family, and the Holy Spirit imparted the nature of Christ within us.

> But He answered them, 'My mother and my brothers
> are those who hear the word of God and do it. (Luke 8:21)

Sounds like family to me!

A family's personality is a mixture of its culture, history, and beliefs, and if it is a close group, the members display, in one way or another, the common traits of the family as a whole. This can be good or bad, maybe even funny. The idea that some people look like their dogs comes to mind.

Despite individual quirks, peculiarities, and preferences, family folk can be identified as having the same character, which has been called the "spirit of the family." Sometimes, our kitchen walls reverberate with laughter and love, as they did on Father's Day when eleven family members and two dogs gathered to celebrate the dads. That's clearly the spirit of our family—loud, affectionate, and very funny. It's as if we have all become one vibrant entertainer, dramatist, or comedian for whatever occasion the stage has been set. Above all, the common bond in our family is our faith. We are intertwined in the Holy Spirit because we belong to the family of God.

The Christian rock band, *Switchfoot* sang it best at a concert I attended a while ago with the younger members of our boisterous family. As the band approached the stage, their opening song was, "We are One Tonight."

Just as a family who gets together at a picnic, football game, or a summer vacation becomes united and displays their common characteristics, so God and His Son, Jesus are one and the Holy Spirit is the result, or character, of their unity. The Holy Spirit is all that Jesus is in His Father. This family of three has become One with very identifiable traits, the best ones for mankind: love, kindness, mercy, power, courage, compassion, humility, and righteousness, to name a few.

Through Jesus' death on the cross, His Father provided a way for us to join God's family and share its identity. Until then, unless we had been of Hebrew descent, we could never have been in the brethren of God's Chosen People. Before Jesus came to show people how His Father wanted us to live and be like Him, God used His power to demonstrate His commandments. God is righteous, and He deemed His people to be so. But they were human—disobedient, wayward, and envious. They needed a role model, someone to emulate . . . better still, a Father they could relate to. God the Father sent His Son, Jesus, to rescue not only the Hebrews but the outsiders as well. He provided for our adoption through His Son and He imparted His Holy Spirit.

In love, He predestined us for adoption as sons [and daughters]
through Jesus Christ according to the purpose of His will...
with which He blessed us in the Beloved. In Him you also when you
heard the word of truth, the gospel of your salvation, and believed in
Him were sealed with the promised Holy Spirit. (Ephesians 1:5–6,13)

How can we remember that the Holy Spirit is in us, even as we chase around, playing life's games? We are family, and we have inherited all of God's gifts, His likeness.

To each is given the manifestation of the Spirit for the common good.
(1 Corinthians 12:7)

When we are in the family of Christ, we have the fruit of the Spirit coursing through our veins—love, joy, peace, patience, kindness, goodness, gentleness, and even, self-control!

. . . for in Christ Jesus, you are all sons [and daughters]
of God, through faith. (Galatians 3:26b)

You, me, and the Church: We are family in the Kingdom of God! As the saying goes, "The apple doesn't fall far from the tree." The power of the Holy Spirit is with us all.

SECTION II
FITNESS

FRUITFUL FITNESS

There was a time I was called "The Terminator" and left my victims behind, huffing and puffing in pools of sweat. Little did those who granted me the lofty title know that I had once been a Fluff Ball . . . and a rather round one at that. As a certified fitness instructor with "Movement is Life" as my mantra, it became my vendetta to walk my talk. I taught exercises with ferocity and fitness with fervor. The Christian Broadcasting Network owned the facility I managed and gave me carte blanche to establish a fitness ministry. Perhaps this is why God allowed me to feel invincible and passionate about the good news of wellness. Yes, with my help, anyone could conquer cellulite, chocolate, and low self-esteem!

And so they came—the weary, weak, and wary—for body fat assessments, weight management programs, and exercise schedules. Most of them were overworked pastors and professionals, stressed-out college students, and exhausted moms, all who had put good habits and personal health on the back burners while giving themselves to God and the all-consuming tasks before them. Some struggled with guilt for neglecting their "temples," and many weighed the consequences of choosing exercise over service. They finally relented and came to the fitness center after learning the exercise music was Christian, they could prop their Bibles on the treadmills, and the membership fee was nominal.

I was a chubby kid—"fat" my mother muttered when my mouth was stuffed with fries, or my bathing suit split at the seams. Ashamed for not being as slim as she had wanted, I later battled my weight and shape intermittently with cottage cheese and celery sticks. In those days, exercise was an assignment, much like writing spelling words or solving arithmetic problems in school workbooks. I didn't exercise in the true sense of the verb until I was thirty when I took up running, hoping to make friends, and the best way to get to know the women who jogged regularly past my house was to join them. So I bought some brown waffle shoes called Nikes and started jogging at night. Through pain, sweat, and sheer grit, I finally managed to wobble myself the one-mile loop around my house. In that struggle, I learned *suffering produces endurance* (Romans 5:3), and *I can do all things through Christ* (Philippians 4:13), as if I had penned the words myself in blood. The accomplishment felt like a crown from heaven. For the first time in my life, I felt strength I had never known, which opened the door to new friendships, a women's Bible study, and miles upon miles of running.

Ten years after jogging my first mile, I had run, swum, jumped, and biked myself into my career in physical fitness and the management of a fitness center. The journey of training, challenges, and pain had not been easy, especially at my age, but I learned the real-life struggle of perseverance. Through these experiences, I realized God wanted all of His children to be at their best physically, as well as spiritually, not only for their own health but also for their unique services in His Kingdom.

How was it that I, in my mid-forties, jumping and running around like a teenager or an aging athlete on steroids, was able to counsel the dejected and deconditioned patrons who came apologetically to my door? I could have been enamored with my own success and brawn or chosen to surround myself with the young and beautiful. My bent could have been to put up a "Manager Not In" sign and go out for a run or sit back to read the latest *Shape Magazine*. Had I rolled my eyes at people who would rather walk than run, whined that the bike seats were too hard, or cringed when sweat rolled down their brows, these poisonous thoughts may have stolen the joys God intended for me, which had nothing to do with a single digit of body fat or running five miles. By reminding me of my past, God rescued me from myself. Instead of becoming a fitness fanatic, I became an advocate for faith, fitness, and fruit.

Blessed is the man who trusts in the Lord, whose trust is the Lord.
He is like the tree planted by water, that sends out its roots
by the stream, and does not fear when heat comes, for its leaves
remain green, and is not anxious in the year of drought,
for it does not cease to bear fruit. (Jeremiah 17:7–8)

This is the picture of health and fitness I described to my clients who sought help. Because of the embarrassment and rejection I had felt when I didn't measure up to the perfect physique, my heart broke when clients told me they had lost hope and didn't think they could ever be healthy or look good again. They thought they were failures, and their biggest enemy was shame. I knew to the depths of my heart how they felt.

I will most gladly spend and be spent for your souls. (2 Corinthians 12:15)

God anointed me with oils of compassion, hope, and encouragement for those defeated souls. I reminded them that God "did not make junk," this was a new season, they would be made new, and their victory had already been won. All they had to do was have faith in their goals, keep moving, and live in the fruit of God's promises.

My heart swells when I remember the folks who learned to jog, attended Step classes and sweated through push-ups and lunges. Their eyes brightened, smiles widened, and spirits lifted as they worked themselves back to the vibrant, purpose-filled lives God had called them to live.

Having once been called The Terminator still makes me chuckle. Being used to "comfort those who are in any affliction" (2 Corinthians 1:4) with God's own comfort as I had been able to do at the fitness center brings me to my knees in humility and wonder. Anyone with a past can be anointed. With God, even a Terminator can offer a new beginning!

DIVERSE EXCELLENCE

Agroup becomes a team when its members set a common goal. The personalities and paradigms of the members may be different, but if their commitment is true, the goal will come to life. Often the variations within can be difficult for the team and create tension. We know this because we've been involved with all sorts of teams at one time or another, and each of us has had to learn to cooperate, bite our tongues, look the other way, and give a little—or a lot—for the common good. A team's ultimate success depends not only on the people but also on the integrity of the goal.

When I was given the task of creating a staff for the fitness center of the Christian Broadcasting Network's five-star hotel, I had never interviewed anyone, let alone checked qualifications, created job descriptions, or determined hourly wages. A stay-at-home mom in my forties, I felt vastly under-qualified. I didn't even know how to operate a photocopy machine. Due largely to my lack of experience, yet true to my nature, I liked everybody who came into my brand-new office and enjoyed letting them interview me. Meanwhile, I prayed like a monk for wisdom and guidance while God assembled His team.

Within a month, my new staff and I asked God for a vision for our fitness center, and together, we prayerfully committed to creating a safe, welcoming environment for guests and clients seeking relaxation, rejuvenation, and restoration through physical fitness. We desired to give God the glory for every victory. With our goal before us, the staff at the Founders Inn Fitness Center became a team.

In spite of the fact we were immersed in a Christian environment and we prayed together at our staff meetings, there were challenges within the ministrations of our fitness endeavor. We were a motley group. A former stay-at-home mom and aerobics instructor, I suddenly found myself in charge of a spirited, stalwart bunch of young adults. Except for our passion for fitness, we could not have been more different from each other.

My first interviewee was so laid back, I wondered if he could push a lawn-mower, let alone lift barbells. He walked slowly, kept to himself, and cared little about his appearance. Why did I hire him? God had told me, "This is your first one." And so he was. For nine years, he managed the registers, cleaned and repaired equipment, worked extra hours, and charmed the hotel guests with his gentle demeanor. He faithfully served the team's goal.

A little while later, I hired a giant of a kid with a smile as wide as his legs were long. He was an athlete and loved children, so he had been an easy pick. He filled our fitness center with gales of high-pitched laughter and delighted us by singing beach rock-n-roll while cleaning the center's pools. Larger than life, he took the team's goal to heart.

Our massage therapist carried a jug of garlic water and knew all about herbs and organic food. We could smell garlic fumes from the therapy room as she vigorously massaged her contented clients. One of our front desk attendants, always eager to help others along their spiritual walks with Jesus, welcomed exercise enthusiasts with a warm smile that soon engaged them in a life-giving conversation.

Over the years, the fitness center thrived, and the staff multiplied and changed. Our new staff members included a muscular Italian dedicated to the expertise of weight training, and a student of theology with endless energy and such passion for fitness he became a magnet of success for our Fitness Center. Everybody loved him, so it was no surprise to any of us when he jaunted through the front door with Dr. Pat Robertson skipping at his heels!

Another one of my employees is a proud grandpa now whom I often see at church beaming with the vitality of good health and an active lifestyle. He had become one of the gym's most fervent cross-trainers, and still humbly claims that his boss, "The Terminator," trained him.

It's not hard to imagine the dynamics pinging off the walls from this diverse group as we created programs, classes, and evaluations for hundreds of people. But what unified us was our mission, which we pursued with passion, gritting our teeth and holding our tongues as we created a ministry of health and fitness.

As we had hoped and prayed, our team's goal had been God's goal all along. We welcomed people to a place where they could become as healthy and strong as He had created them to be. This was His victory, not ours.

A team whose members are committed to its goal can be successful in our world of diversity, and this is a sweet victory. But the team whose goals are first committed to God joins His higher team's purpose: that of bringing victory to a diversified world and giving Him all the glory.

Let's see how inventive we can be in encouraging love and helping out, not avoiding worship together as some do but spurring each other on as we see the big Day approaching. (Hebrews 10:24–25, MSG)

MOVEMENT IS LIFE

The story of Gideon and the less than stellar history of the Israelites found in the pages of the Book of Judges is one about movement. Due to their habitual, almost predictable disobedience to God, His Chosen People had once again found themselves in bondage to a cruel and oppressive force, the Midianites.

Like the tides of the ocean, the people's passion for God and His ways ebbed and flowed with their needs of the moment and the tempting idols surrounding them. Over and over, they drifted away from the explicit commands of God and His provision to become embroiled and overcome by the enemies surrounding them. Then in fearful desperation, they cried out to God and, like a great wave, ran to Him, repenting all the way.

We are like those fickle Israelites when we let the circumstances of our lives—demanding bills, schedules, relationships, kids, yard work, car repairs, jobs—pull us away from God. In His fatherly love, God allows the enemy of stress, tension, and exhaustion to mow us down until we are weak and limp, only able to whine, "Please God, help me out of this mess."

In Gideon's day, the situation was worse than destruction from a great tidal wave. For seven years, the enemy had so overpowered God's children that they were forced to exist in mountain dens and caves. All of their resources were plundered in the land where they were trapped. Their lives had become stagnant.

Sometimes life is overwhelming. We feel stuck in our mess. Depression, boredom, and exhaustion set in. Or we've reached the top of our careers and obtained the goals we had set and begin to wonder if there is anything else. There seems to be nothing on the horizon. It's as if we are floating still in stagnant water, going nowhere. Just as it had been for the Israelites trapped in their holes, it can be easy for us to forget our hope.

Where there is no vision, the people perish. (Proverbs 29:18)

"Movement is life" has been my mantra since my early career as a personal trainer. Moving meant burning calories. Now, dealing with a lot of arthritis and a little bit of aging, I find life is better when I can move. Forget about the calories. God created us to move. Movement *gives* life.

So it happened that Gideon found himself hiding in an old rugged winepress. But instead of licking grape juice from his sandals or snoozing until nightfall when he could change positions, Gideon kept himself busy.

. . .Gideon was beating out wheat in the wine press
to hide it from the Midianites. (Judges 6:11)

Rather than whining and complaining about being cramped in a dank vat, Gideon found a way to make wheat to feed his family and friends. He used his trap to give life!

When I see people who are physically challenged and bound to a wheel-chair, walker, or even a cane, my heart weeps for their immobility. But then I marvel how, in spite of the challenges, they are out and about, shopping, attending church, playing sports, leading motivational groups, and enjoying life. These are the people I call heroes, the ones who inspire me by their tenacity and joy. These folks aren't sitting around having a pity party. As Gideon did, they make life worth living wherever they are.

The angel of the Lord came, sat down under a tree, and watched Gideon busily beat away the chaff. At last, He had found someone producing something in the desolate land, making hope an action word. It is no wonder the angel declared, "The Lord is with you, O mighty man of valor." (Judges 6:12)

When we think we have been abandoned by God in a hopeless situation, even the smallest movement toward something good—watering the garden, cleaning the bathroom, washing the car, or writing a note of gratitude—will bring God's legions of angels to your rescue, all proclaiming, "THE LORD IS WITH YOU!" But you must move first.

Gideon, the obscure man of action with no medals or background check, had just been selected by God Himself to free the starving stagnant people sitting in caves. The first question he asked was, "What about them?" He demanded to know why all this persecution had come upon God's people when the stories of their forefathers had promised God's deliverance. Gideon did not ask for his rescue, a suit of armor, or a new condo. He wanted to be sure God was paying attention to the plight of everyone else. The Lord assured him, "Go in this might of yours and save Israel from the hand of Midian." (Judges 6:14)

John Mason, a renowned Christian motivator, once said, "The first step toward going somewhere is to decide that you are not going to stay where you are."

Our God is a God of motion, and He intends for us to move with Him. To stay put looking and cringing at the world around us is a sure means to death. God is moving forward with purpose, progress, and promises in His plan for His kingdom. Just as He called Gideon to move out and be a warrior, He is calling us to move and live and be in Him.

> Yet He is actually not far from each one of us, for in Him
> we move and live and have our being . . . (Acts 17:28)

THE AARON AND HUR IN YOU

While the Israelites were trying to get used to depending upon God for their needs, complaining more than coping, they were confronted by yet another challenge.

The formerly enslaved people were just learning to enjoy their families, move about with their friends, and relax, when some unfriendly neighbors, the warring Amalekites, threatened to attack. As slaves in Egypt, the Israelites had no training in warfare. The Egyptian armies fought and conquered other territories, while the oppressed Israelites were starved and whipped as they built bricks, roads, and cities. Now, they had to organize their own fighting army. Can you imagine the terror? Who would be their general and where would they get weapons?

Just when we think we've figured out this faith walk with God and we get a teensy bit comfortable, a new unexpected problem gets us up from the easy chair. After the initial shock and wailing, this is when we pray harder and reach for our Bibles.

Moses reached for his staff, which, at God's command, had changed from a stick to a snake, turned the waters of the Nile to blood, and blasted frogs, locusts, gnats, flies, and hail upon the stubborn Egyptians. Moses remembered the power of God that had been in his staff and knew he would need it for the oncoming fight. God's Word is the weapon we must use to overcome the battles we face on a daily basis. The Bible is our staff of choice!

Moses chose Joshua from among the Israelites to form the army to defeat the Amalekites. Most likely, he prayed about this grave selection to best prepare the

80

new army for battle. Joshua's leadership skills and commitment to God were superior, and he eventually became Moses's successor, leading Israel into the Promised Land. The Israelites had a general!

How do we know if we make the right choice about a move, a doctor, an investment, or any other important decision? As the stress of the impending matter rises, we must give our decision to God, as Moses did, and go into the fray. We have to trust our prayer instincts, channeled by God through our faith, and remember that He never makes a mistake.

Scripture does not tell us if God directed Moses to carry his staff to a nearby hill above the raging battle. Most generals would seek such a vantage point to oversee the fight. But it makes sense that Moses took his staff rather than a sword or bow because he had confidence in the power of God. He would wave it above his head to remind Joshua's army of God's presence. He had seen that power before. So with his brother Aaron, the prophet, and Hur, a brave friend who was willing to join them, the great leader went to the top of the hill and raised "the rod of God."

You and I have done the same thing, haven't we? When the battles we fight rage, we raise our hands to God and cry out for an end to the struggles. Sometimes, the hardship and strife go on and on, so we reach deeper into our faith and pray harder. It is exhausting, but we know God sees and hears our longings and petitions. We cry out to the Lord, "Victory, please!"

Whenever Moses raised his great staff, he saw the Amalekites retreat, and when he brought the staff down to switch hands, the enemy attacked the Israeli forces with vengeance. Moses would then push the heavy staff up again, and Joshua's army would claim a victory.

Can you imagine Moses's exhaustion and desperate prayers? When have you felt worn out by fear, pain, or anxiety? Have you wondered how you would be able to go on? Like me, have you ever cried out to God, "I'm *done*! This is too much for me!"

Before Moses had a chance to toss his staff, Aaron and Hur had an idea. They rolled a stone and put it under their leader. Possibly Hur, the quiet one, said, "Here, Mo, sit on this." And Moses sat on the rock.

The ache in his back, cramping in his legs, and throbbing in his feet left as Moses relaxed on his rock. He could breathe again, think more clearly, and pray quietly.

We have a Rock, and He is Jesus Christ. Just as He was with Moses and the Israelites, pouring forth water for survival, so He is with us, offering Living Water. We can fall on the Rock of Jesus, drape ourselves all over Him, and drink in His love. He is there.

As Moses regained his strength on the stone, Aaron and Hur, one at each side, held up the hand grasping the mighty staff. Until the end of the day, they helped Moses raise his staff and kept his arms steady.

And Joshua overwhelmed Amalek and his people with the sword.
(Exodus 17:13)

Who holds you up when you are weary? This is when we most need our church family. When we think we can't carry anymore, we need our Christian brothers and sisters to come to us with blessings, encouragement, and prayer. Food, yard work, and babysitters go a long way, too.

When we are able, or even if we don't think we are, we, too, can do uplifting deeds for others. We don't have to be great leaders like Moses or warriors like Joshua to win the battle against doubt and despondency. We are all Aarons and Hurs for people in need. Just go up the hill to the one God has sent you and, on the Rock of Jesus, help lift the burden.

DIRTY CLOTHES AND CLEAN CHAMPION

When Simon Peter heard that it was the Lord, he put on his outer
garment, for he was stripped for work, and threw himself into the sea.
(John 7:7b)

Have you ever felt so humiliated, ashamed, or trapped in your own
self-abasement that you wanted to dig a hole, climb into it, and let the
dirt fall over you? Maybe you've felt so angry with yourself about something you did or didn't do, said, or got caught in the middle of—something
downright ugly—and you wanted to rip off your clothes, tear out your hair, or
just jump ship.

That's what Simon Peter did. After turning his back on Jesus, he tore off his
clothes and went fishing. Peter wasn't an athlete; he was a fisherman who had
given up his trade and the life he knew for the only Man in his life that had
enough patience to keep him focused on a mission.

Jesus just wanted Peter to pay attention and listen to His words, not the
voices in his head. If only the emotional disciple would slow down and watch
what Jesus was doing instead of jumping ahead, trying to do everything better,
bigger, and faster. At one point, Jesus told His floundering disciple that He had to
pray for him so his "faith would not fail."

The fisherman was all heart and no head. It was so easy for him to get distracted trying to please everyone.

Lord, I'm ready to go with you to prison and to death! Less than twelve hours later, he declared, "Woman, I do not know him! (Luke 22:33,57)

Trying to please Jesus or be Jesus can be the same as denying Jesus.

When he saw the Messiah tortured and crucified, Peter finally came undone. "I am going fishing."

We have all been there. Made such a mess of things that there's no way out. Egg on the face, hand in the cookie jar.

Out at sea in the boat, far away from his blunders, Peter stripped off his clothes and got to work in his skivvies (I imagine). Those other clothes smelled of the past—lies, cowardice, and murder. He'd been dressed in that stench long enough, and now, he wanted nothing to do with it. Peter lost himself in his fishing. Unfortunately, he was practically naked and there were no fish.

"Nobody wants me anyway, not even fish."

Only One Person wants us in the "Nobody-wants-me-everybody-hates-me" state of mind. Jesus wants us all—the winners and woebegoners, alike. He doesn't see our mistakes; He sees our potential for the Kingdom of God.

At the shoreline, The Resurrected Lord called out to the fishermen, including Peter, His clumsy champion of sorts. Pulling on his old stinky clothes, impetuous, passionate, pathetic Peter jumped into the ocean and swam to shore to his beloved Friend. Can you imagine how heavy those clothes were in the water and how they must have dragged down the desperate swimmer? Peter wanted Jesus so badly that he threw himself out to sea and hauled his waterlogged clothes through the waves to get to Him. By the time he reached the sand where Jesus was waiting (smiling no doubt), Peter had been washed clean.

That was the third time Peter and Jesus had been separated by water. Sometimes, it takes us a few times to really get it.

The first time, Jesus stood on the waves of a stormy sea and called Peter to come to Him. Peter jumped over the side of the boat and started walking until he realized where he was, became afraid, lost his focus, and sunk. The second time, he and Jesus had a conversation over the water with which Jesus used to wash the disciples' feet. Pete insisted that as long as Jesus was at it, his hands and head could use washing, as well. This third time, Peter saw Jesus on the other side of the water, and he had to defy all of the elements Satan used to keep him from the Messiah. Peter had to wrench free of fear, pride, and shame.

Simon the fisherman, renamed Peter the Rock by the Messiah, swam clean to redemption.

"Do you love me, Peter?" Jesus asked three times.

"You know that I love You!" Of course, Peter cried.

With the weighted tenderness of a wise Master, Jesus reminded His faithful friend that the clothes he had been wearing were those he had chosen, and he had been able to go wherever he wanted. As a follower of Jesus, he would be dressed by another and carried to where he did not want to go. Peter would sacrifice his life to glorify God.

"Follow Me," Jesus said. And Peter did.

THE SOUND OF GOD'S SILENCE

O swald Chambers wrote, "God's silences are actually His answers." Now that is an arresting thought. Was Chambers being sarcastic? Most of us feel neglected, rejected, and pitiful when we don't get answers or results from our prayers. When God doesn't deliver, we don't understand. How could His silence be His answer?

I have never thought of my ongoing problems as a way of understanding better the sovereignty of God. Yet, when I pull away from my frustration or despair and actually trust Him in the moment, I sense His Spirit. God is answering my prayer, just not on my schedule.

By waiting for God's timing to answer our prayers when it feels like nothing at all is happening, we are actually growing in faith.

In the eleventh chapter of the book of John, we read that Mary and Martha's brother, Lazarus, is near death, and they send an urgent message to their dear friend, Jesus, saying, "Lord, he whom You love is ill" (John 11:3).

How like our own prayers this is!

"Jesus, I know You love me, so bring-fix-heal-ANSWER my prayer!" And like Martha and Mary, we wait. And wait.

> Now Jesus loved Martha and her sister and Lazarus.
> So, when He heard that Lazarus was ill, He stayed
> two days longer in the place where He was. (John 11:5–6)

86

Can you imagine the agony the sisters felt as they watched their brother slip slowly away from them, and still Jesus, their only hope, did not show up? Did they know that Jesus would heal Lazarus, or did they think the love between the two friends would revive him? All we know is that their brother died, and Jesus had not even sent a message.

When I spent two months gripped and trapped by back spasms, and I prayed. Oh, how I prayed for relief, mercy, and strength. God was silent, it seemed. Enduring the pain, taking the medicine, and altering my activities, I waited for God to answer my prayers. Ultimately, the pain subsided and once again, as if I had never waited a moment, I knew the sovereign grace of God.

"This illness does not lead to death. It is for the glory of God, so that the Son of God may be glorified through it." (Verse 4)

The promises of God to His beloved are active and true, coming to us from a totally different time zone than ours. As we wait and pray, the glory of God pierces our understanding, shatters our despair, and astonishes us with revelation. In His silence, God's glory is formed in our understanding.

My seven-year-old granddaughter and namesake, Meredith, gave me a clear illustration of how God hears and answers our prayers. I was with her this weekend as she waited for my daughter, her "Bear Bear," as all the cousins affectionately call their Aunt Kerith, to come for a visit. With well-worn wisdom, Meredith's mother had waited until the morning of Bear Bear's arrival to tell her daughter the news, for she knew that her child would find waiting for her beloved aunt unbearable. Actually, her impatience was painful for all of us. Every minute throughout the day, Meredith asked, "Is she here? Is she here?" even though she could see out the same window as we could that no car had been driven into the driveway. Still, she begged, whined, and demanded, "Where *is* she? When will she be here? You PROMISED!"

Yes, we had promised and, barring an unforeseen mishap, Aunt Kerith would arrive as soon as she traveled the two hundred miles to get there. But Meredith didn't know this. She only knew of her need for *right now* because we had promised that Bear Bear was coming.

This is how God answers our prayers. First, He is good for His promise. He *will* come to us. Second, He will show Himself to us when the hour is right. His "travel time" is different than ours. His is not an estimated time of arrival, an ETA. God comes when there are no more miles to travel, only the place of His arrival—His answer.

Finally, Bear Bear's car pulled up in front of the house. Meredith's ecstasy was electric; it seemed as if she was surprised that we had kept our promise. She screamed, jumped, laughed, and cried, throwing herself at her aunt. All of the waiting, doubting, and longing was gone, and only joy filled the moment!

When God answers our prayers, and He does, we forget the delay. The silence is filled with the glory of Him who has done it.

And Jesus lifted up His eyes and said,
'Father, I thank You that You have heard me.' (John 11:41)

TRUST YOU CAN SLEEP ON

fear I am beginning to lose my balance on the mountaintop. Is the pain returning?

It wasn't long ago when I went to the doctor and begged for cortisone. The inflammation in my hands and shoulders was unbearable, and I felt physically, emotionally, and spiritually undone. This was a familiar pit from which God had pulled me time and time again, and I was overdue for rescue. Would He hear my cries again?

> He drew me up from the pit of destruction, out of the miry bog . . .
> (Psalm 40:2)

Peter was in quite a pit himself when Herod had him thrown in jail, chained and guarded by four sentries for the night. He had seen this ominous behavior by Herod before (Acts 12).

The pit had a familiar scent. The disciples had been sought out, one was killed, and the other, Peter, thrown in jail until after Passover, to be tried the next day. All of the disciples remembered the day their Messiah had been sentenced to die on the cross. Peter needed rescue, but the probabilities didn't look good. He was chained between two guards.

Our miry pits can take on recognizable décor. The abyss of despair, the cave of shame, the ditch of self-pity, and the prison of fear are places we all have been before. It is here that Satan steals our focus, robs our confidence, and undermines our trust. He even makes us grumpy.

I was a grump on steroids by the time I got to my doctor. "This is not me," I wailed. "Fix me!" The place I was so miserable was not in the pain I felt, it was the loss of hope. Was this it for me? Was I to be crippled forever, trapped in a vise of pain? God had brought me so far in the battle with rheumatoid arthritis and given me peace, patience, and even wisdom as I lost more and more of my former active life, the one I had depended on. Now, I needed His grace more than ever.

What does grace look like in times of trial? We see it in so many ways we often don't recognize it. I think of grace as God's love shining bright in the smiles of people who are weary, cashiers and waiters who are friendly, strangers who are helpful, soldiers who comfort one another, and especially my young friend battling cancer who sends out her smiling picture before her treatments.

Grace is God's peace, joy, and love in the midst of trouble. In Peter's case, chained in jail, grace looked like sleep, and he slept so hard the angel who had come to rescue him had to hit him to wake him up. Like a baby with its blanket, Peter slept with his trust in God, not in fear of the prison. How is it that he could sleep so peacefully, chained, most likely, to his death sentence?

Peter had been on several mountaintops with His Lord. He was invited by Jesus to join Him, James, and John to the mountain where he actually heard God's voice at the transfiguration (Mark 9). Later, Jesus gave Peter his first lesson in trust by calling him to walk on water (Matthew 14:28–29). When Peter was pitched into a dark hole of guilt from denying his relationship with Jesus, he was lifted out by the Risen Messiah, who told him personally, "Feed my sheep," and "Follow me" (John 21:15–18).

From his mountaintop experiences, Peter's spiritual thinking matured. He was filled with the Holy Spirit and became a bold speaker, healer, and leader of the first Christian church. But Peter did not revel in the glory of his spiritual successes; he lived them out as he witnessed to hundreds of people, bringing them into the knowledge of Jesus Christ.

Oswald Chambers wrote, "Living a life of faith means not knowing where you are being led. It is a life of knowing Him who calls us to go." Remaining on the mountaintop is not an option but taking the revelation from it is our responsibility.

My doctor gave me the shot of cortisone I needed and within days, I enjoyed mobility, energy, and freedom from pain. I began to climb a mountain of renewal and rejoicing, feeling my hand in God's. I knew the medicine could last about a month or two, so I wanted to be filled with as much joy as God would give me and walk in His grace, even if the pain came back.

I am not slipping off of my mountaintop, and you will not slip off yours. We will go where God calls us, even if it hurts.

C.S. Lewis reminds us in his book, *The Problem with Pain*, "Our Father refreshes us on the journey with some pleasant inns but will not encourage us to mistake them for home."

We can leave our hiatus filled with new trust in a sovereign God who already has our next mountaintop planned. Like Peter who slept in prison and was rescued, we will learn to rest in the One Who has "turned for me my mourning into dancing . . . have loosed my sackcloth and clothed me with gladness, that my glory may sing Your praise."

O Lord my God, I will give thanks to You forever! (Psalm 30:11–12)

METAPHOR MAKEOVER

O nce in a great while, I treat myself to a makeover. I rationalize the pampering as a favor to my fans, e.g., my long-suffering husband who gently reminds me that beauty is of "a quiet and gentle spirit" (1 Peter 3:4, NIV), my two schnauzers, each of whom has their preference of lotion flavors, and my magnifying mirror, which is blatantly unforgiving. A girl must do what she must do.

The transformation to my face is most desperately needed in late winter when my complexion turns ice-grey, my pupils disappear, my lips pucker inversely, and the wrinkles out-number the mirror's water spots. Surely there is hope in a bottle, powder, or mascara wand. So with a bag over my head, I head to the mall to find a miracle worker behind the cosmetics counter. Never mind this face-paint professional is twenty—no, thirty—years younger than me, has a complexion like my eight-month-old granddaughter, eyes shaded, shadowed, and sparkling like Monet's "Water Lilies," and shimmering Cindy Lou Who lips, she is my BFF for the hour or two it takes her to do something new and miraculous to my face. Truth is, I need a change; the reality is I would need to be thirty years younger. My life for the moment is in her hands. Bless her heart.

My attitude toward the New Year already needs a radical makeover. With a mantle of six-plus decades draped on my shoulders, a season of holidays, football games, national elections, family drama tickling my nerves, and a culmination of unparalleled world tragedies dragging my heart, it will take more than a shower to remove the residue of the past in order to put on a bright face for the future.

Do not remember the former things of old. Nor consider the things
of old. Behold I will do a new thing. (Isaiah 43:18-19)

How can I envision a "new thing"? I am worn out by the old stuff. The other day I perused my previous year's journal, my annual ritual of looking for God's handprint on the pages of my scribbled observations, opinions, and prayers. Much to my chagrin, I read a surprising amount of whining. Yes, I confess it. Between the blessings, healings, revelations, and answered prayer, I also complained, questioned, and wailed at God. Even when I recorded wisdom from God's Word and paraphrased passages of Scripture, my own distasteful words of self-pity, impatience, and despair sprinkled the pages of my journal. I'd really hoped to do a better job last year. What would keep me from bringing more of the same attitude to the New Year?

If anyone is in Christ, (s)he is a new creation;
old things have passed away; the new has come. (2 Corinthians 5:17)

The Greek word for new, *kainos*, refers to "new, unused, and fresh," in regard to form or quality rather than time. So according to Paul, if we are in Christ, we are fresh, spanking *new* all of the time! No looking back or dragging old baggage.

I've been in need of a Metaphor Makeover! I must erase last year's record of failures, fears, and regrets. My overused metaphor of perfection and peace for a New Year has already run out of warranty; God has given me a gift card that is eternal.

This new metaphor is reality: I am in Christ. He is my identity, standard, measure, and purpose. In Christ, I have joy, hope, peace, and love—perfection. I am free of self-destructive thinking and hope-defeating fears. My God is doing a *new* thing, and I am included. I can trust Him in all things as I embark upon the New Year.

For the Lord will go before you, and the God of Israel
will be your rear guard. (Isaiah 52:12)

God is the God of our yesterdays and our tomorrows. It is in Him we must trust, not in our idea of what He should do or what we think He expects. While He may use the mistakes we made last year as lessons for spiritual growth, He will not use them as hammers. We do not have to be afraid of the future, ashamed of our past, or covering our heads with bags to hide the wear and tear. We are free to be all that He is in us. This is a makeover worth pursuing forever!

LOVE DEEPLY

"Love deeply," Peter wrote in his first epistle, and Peter would know. Loving with affection is natural; loving with compassion is grace; loving deeply from the soul is a mystery. How does one love deeply? How did Peter know?

Thanks to Gary Chapman who wrote the book, *The Five Love Languages* to help us identify each other's unique love instinct, we can sort out and become aware of our emotions when giving or needing love. Some of us like presents; others appreciate a Starbucks café date or receiving snail mail. There are those who glow from affirmation as they accomplish goals never expected by the one who appreciates the work being done. Of course, there is the lover of touch, and I think God gave all of us a bit, if not a barrelful, of that love language.

Peter could have written to the Gentiles, the Christian newbies unfamiliar with the charitable commandments of Leviticus (25:35–44), about loving generously, unselfishly, or even honestly. But Peter's message points to people of all ages and in all ages about our attitude toward others. We are to love deeply, charitably, and fervently because only in this way can we demolish all hindrances to trustworthy relationships.

Is this possible? How do we love others and do so completely unhindered by our own human flaws? I struggle with this daily, almost hourly. I even fail miserably trying to like those drivers on the expressway who pass me on the right. I also feel a little huffy in the grocery store when I'm trying to get around someone standing near the middle of the aisle perusing a double-thick binder of coupons. These are minor irritations—we all have pet peeves that pinch our perfect hearts.

What really breaks my heart and keeps it shallow are the insidious critical thoughts that line up behind my disapproving eye, the sarcastic word that escapes before I can squelch it, or the pity pit I jump into the moment I feel misunderstood, maligned, or mismanaged. It is true, isn't it, that our natural hearts want presents, kindness, success, purpose, hugs, or usually all five! To love deeply without expectation is supernatural and sacrificial.

Peter exhorted genuine no-strings-attached love because this is the love he had received from Jesus. He knew too well from his own past experiences that he was not capable of loving as Jesus loved. He had made too many mistakes, big mistakes even with the Son of God. Until he knew in his heart of hearts that Jesus loved him enough to forgive him, Peter did not know love at all. Temper, impatience, arrogance, betrayal—who could love a sinner with those characteristics? Like Peter. How could a sinner like that love anyone else? Not Peter.

It is really hard to be kind, caring, and compassionate with strangers or our spouses when squirming under the hammer we use to hit ourselves with after uttering an insensitive slur, complaining about somebody's need, or cutting in line in front of children at the movies. How can we love if we are not loveable? Sometimes it's comfortable in an achy sort of way to feel unloved; there's no need to love back.

What if Peter had stayed out on that fishing boat, stripped to his skivvies, groaning and moaning about no fish, friends, or faith, and never looked up to see that bright beckoning face on the shore (John 21:1–8)? He could have jumped overboard and drowned himself in self-hatred while his buddies took the boat to the beach for a fish barbecue with the Savior. Instead, Peter got over himself and looked to shore. Jesus Christ had forgiven him. He knew it deep in his heart. He threw on his old clothes and swam to the One who loved Him enough to forget all his faults, and when he got to shore, he was filled with a love that only Jesus could put in his heart.

"Do you love Me?" Jesus asked Peter three times over, making sure Peter responded with the forgiveness kind of love—love without guilt, shame, or condemnation. This is deep love. It is the only miraculous way that we can love others; it's a way that covers "a multitude of sins." We must first know we are forgiven and adored by God our Father, in spite of every blunder, bust, or baleful thought we have had in our past . . . even since this morning.

"Lord, you know everything; You know that I love You." (John 21:17)

Yes, Jesus knew that Peter loved Him because He does know all things. But the important thing was for *Peter* to know that he loved Jesus and had been found faithful in spite of his flaws. Jesus knew He could trust Peter to "feed My sheep," and Peter had to know he could trust Jesus within him to carry out the greatest act of charity the world would ever know.

Before we can serve effectively in the Kingdom of God, we must fully grasp the redeeming Love of Christ.

This is my command: Love one another the way I loved you.
This is the best way to love. (John 15:12–13, MSG)

Jesus' love for all of us was nothing less than sacrificial. He lay down His life so that we may know His Love every time we get over ourselves and get back to Him. His love banishes every sin holding us back from giving to others the same love that He bestows upon us. It is a miraculous love.

May He grant you to be strengthened with power through His Spirit in your inner being so that Christ may dwell in your hearts through faith—that you, being rooted and grounded in love, may have the strength to comprehend with all the saints what is the breadth and length and height and depth, and to know the love of Christ (Ephesians 3:16–19)

"Love deeply," Peter wrote. He knew we must first start from the heart of Christ within us.

SLEEP WELL, BELOVED

With God's help, we can forgive others for what they have done to us and be graciously removed from damaging bitterness. The real battle, though, is letting go of our sins. So often, even after we have confessed and repented, we hold onto our deeds as if we think they are too dirty or dangerous for heaven. What keeps us tossing, turning, and smothering under our pillows at night is not trying to forgive the world for what it has done to us but forgiving ourselves for what we have done to the world.

What a travesty, this self-loathing. How is it that we can grasp the importance of forgiving other people of their wrongdoings, yet buried in the deep recesses of our minds are our secrets of deceit and dysfunction? We are so afraid others may know we yell at our kids regularly, we have no money in savings, we bad-mouth other drivers, we lost our kids' birth certificates, and we secretly joined Weight Watchers—again. We are petrified that people we want as our friends may learn that we've been selfish, dishonest, a bit promiscuous, jealous, and even delirious. We sip Fire Ball, go bowling on Thanksgiving Day, dislike camping, worship with Switchfoot's music, and turn up the volume *at our age* to listen to Pink. Anytime, we might be found out and kicked out.

We break our own hearts over our failing faith, plaguing memories, wrecking fears, and ongoing longing for someone to understand us, knowing no one in the universe ever could. We are just too messy and unworthy, and we've said some pretty awful things to our spouses. So we don't sleep and, behind closed doors, we cry and believe bad things about ourselves. These are strongholds, and God wants to release us.

Henri Nouwen wrote, "One of the tragedies of life is that we forget who we are."

"You are your own worst enemy," my mother used to tell me. Though I'm certain now she meant only to ward off my fears, in God's eyes this admonishment could not have been farther from the truth.

For You formed my inward parts, you knitted me in my mother's womb, I praise you for I am fearfully and wonderfully made. (Psalm 139:13–14)

In Christ, we are "made new." We are:

- *"God's child" (John 1:12)*
- *"God's workmanship" (Ephesians 2:10)*
- *"Christ's friend" (John 15:15)*
- *"A member of Christ's body" (1 Coritnthians 12:27)*
- *"Established, anointed, and sealed by God" (2 Corinthians 1:21–22)*
- *"Holy and blameless" (Ephesians 1:4)*
- *"Forgiven" (Ephesians 1:8)*
- *"Purposeful" (Ephesians 1:9)*
- *"A saint" (Ephesians 1:8)*
- *"Blameless" (1 Corinthians 1:8)*
- *"Victorious" (1 Corinthians 15:57),* and
- *"Chosen and dearly loved" (Colossians 3:12)*

If this is my "enemy," I want her on my side!

God's Word is living, current, and true. If we believe it at all, how can we torture our precious minds and bodies with self-loathing thoughts of guilt, shame, and remorse? We ask for forgiveness yet struggle to receive it. When we pray the Lord's Prayer to "Forgive us our trespasses as we forgive the trespasses of others," many of us cannot embrace our obedience as God's promise to forgive us.

The Lord is merciful and gracious,
slow to anger and abundant in steadfast love.
He will not always chide, nor will He keep His anger forever.
He does not deal with us according to our sins,
nor repay us according to our iniquities.
For as high as the heavens are above the earth,
so great is His steadfast love toward those who fear Him;
as far as the east is from the west,
so far does He remove our transgressions from us.
(Psalm 103:8–12)

Unlike the Old Testament Hebrews, we do not have to stand in a bucket of blood with carcasses of perfect goats, rams, and lambs all around us, trying desperately to be forgiven for every sin we ever thought of or didn't think of. God loves us so fiercely that He did away with all of the bloody sacrificial rituals required by sinful people. He gave us His Son, whose blood was the final sacrifice for our sins. We are not our own enemy: we have been forgiven.

Do I not hate those who hate you, O Lord?
And do I not loathe those who rise up against you?
I hate them with complete hatred;
I count them my enemies. (Psalm 139:21–22)

These are the enemy: doubt, depression, and despair. The hateful sneering voices in our heads, reminding us over and over we are frumpy, flawed, failure-ridden specimen, that enemy keeping us awake at night and making us grumpy in the morning.

Just as we have to learn to separate the doer from the deed when we forgive the acts of persons toward us, we must separate ourselves from the liar who wishes death upon us. We must hate those lies like God hates them, with a "heavenly hatred" completely, victoriously, and finally.

Search me, O God, and know my heart!
Try me and know my thoughts!
And see if there be any grievous way in me,
and lead me into the way everlasting. (Psalm 139: 23–24)

God loves you and me. He wants nothing to separate us from Him and His love. Give Him those grievous thoughts of yours and get a good night's sleep.

You *are* forgiven.

FLASHLIGHT

Recently, I've been praying a lot about letting go of my fears and trusting God. This came about during a late evening bike ride my husband and I took through a campground lit with Christmas lights. It was dark enough that what I could not see prevented me from enjoying the decorations. Although my husband pointed his flashlight on our path as he steered his bike in front of me, he told me after our perilous ride, "You rode so close you might as well have just ridden on my back wheel!"

Yes, it's true. Despite the dazzling Christmas displays lining our way, my eyes were glued to the path in front of the flashlight!

That flashlight, secured in my husband's hand, reminded me of how God had led the Israelites in the vast wilderness, leaving behind the vicious Egyptians.

By day, the Lord went before them by day in a pillar of cloud to lead them along the way, and by night a pillar of fire to give the light. (Exodus 13:21)

What a welcome sight that "pillar of fire" must have been to the massive group of people trying to find its way across a great, wild wilderness in the pitch-black night. Roaring winds, lashing storms, nor pounding rain ever put out that fire. Wherever they set up camp after a long arduous day of travel, as the night settled around them, the fire of God brightened the sky, a reassuring sign of His love.

God's love is like a hefty flashlight in a loved one's hand. It doesn't have to be physical darkness; it can also be a darkness felt deep in the soul. His love is a bright light, maybe not typically sensed in an over-sized flashlight, swirling flames, or a roaring fire (although my grandson claims he has perceived God in many a campfire), but in the eyes of those who know Jesus.

I am the light of the world. Whoever follows me will not walk in darkness but will have the light of life. (John 8:12)

I was stuck in a wilderness of my own last week. While men were in our bathroom doing the plastering part of our renovation, I lay in a bed down the hall, miserable and in pain. I had taken my medicine, turned on the heating pad, and prayed the zillionth time for healing. The whirring heat fans and *slap-swish* of plaster scrapers made sleep impossible. I changed my prayer requests to grace. I just didn't want to lose it with strangers in my house. Eventually, I rested and the pain quieted.

Still shaken but feeling so much better, I went to check the progress in the bathroom. I was not a pretty sight in my PJ's and boasting a bedhead, in serious need of my own renovation. Around the corner, in the skeleton of what used to be our bathroom, was a tall man in white clothing and white powder covering his dark skin. He looked like a ghost emerging from the dark or an angel arising from the depths. He turned to me, his eyes framed in white.

"Hello, ma'am." His smile was brighter than the plaster. "Are you feeling better?"

"Yes, thank you." I actually felt good. But how had he known? I looked into his eyes, and I knew.

"Have you been praying for me?"

"Oh, yes, ma'am. I have. I've been prayin' all morning. I'm Vincent, and I'm a prayin' man!"

The Presence of God blazed bright in my new bathroom!

If we love Christ, His love is in us, shining out like a beacon, no matter who we are or where we are. That love brings joy, hope, and healing into this world, and it is the light we carry. Just as God covered His children with a pillar of fire in the nighttime wilderness, my husband's flashlight directed our way in the dark, and Vincent's prayers eased my pain.

In Him was life and the life was the light of man. The light shines in the darkness, and the darkness has not overcome it. (John1:4–5)

CLOSET HUSBANDS

The story of the Samaritan woman who met Jesus at the well can be haunting. Like this woman who had secret relationships, we all have sins we would rather not talk about. In many ways, we can identify with her. Yes, there are days when we, too, feel beaten down and plain worn out. We just want a fresh start, like a glass of cool water, and all we get is the stale repetition of every day failure. *Just leave us alone.*

She goes to the well, as we do to our corners, to sulk. The Man just needs to move on. She doesn't want to talk to anyone. Like her, we don't want to pray. There is nothing more to say. Asking for help is hopeless. There have been way too many mistakes, grudges, and pain. We have nothing more to give. Our well is dry. Why is He asking *us* for water? We cringe at His request. Our faith is frazzled.

Even if we could give Him water, it would be contaminated with our filth. Our faith is fatigued. We thought we knew what God wanted from us and for the longest time, we had tried so hard to be good. The Samaritan woman's faith in the God of Jacob had given her the same dry results as our efforts to please God. Why?

We have been drinking from the wrong well.

> The woman said to Him, "Sir, give me this water, so I will not
> have to be thirsty or have to come here to draw water." (John 4:15)

Fresh water? Revival? Sure, everyone can use a fresh start, a new attitude, or a kick in the behind. But everything is the same. We stand at the well again.

"What, Jesus, can You do for me now?" we whine. How in the world can He refresh the mess we are in?

His gentle hospitality is arresting. He invites the woman to bring her husband for His Living Water.

"I have no husband!" The woman is shaken and confused. So are we. What sins are we so aligned with that we are stuck in their control, like she in her bad relationships? Who has been sharing in the great pity party?

"You are right—you have had five husbands and you are living with a man now." Sounds like this Samaritan gal has had quite the party herself. The truth stings and exposes what we all try so hard to hide. What the Savior knows reveals the sins that have us trapped.

Like our friend from Samaria, I have been bound to "husbands" of my own.

The one with the strongest hold of all is pride. How devious pride is to make me think I must be more perfect, better than everyone else, always smiling, out-host the other hostesses, and hide my age with more mascara and exercise. How tightly I have clung to this arrogant, vain companion so that I can measure up to the world's standards.

The second "husband" taunts me. It makes me afraid that people think I am dumb, dramatic, or delusional. Fear has a great time pulling me into the belief that I am not creative, just a little crazy. "Stay home with me!" fear implores, trying to convince me to stay close and avoid adventures or new experiences. "You're too old to dance! Too fragile to take risks! Too slow to play!" I am reminded over and over.

I have also lived with judgment, which loves to hook up with pride. It's easy for me to recognize judgment as I raise my eyebrow when I see young women wearing short skirts, ones I wish I could wear, hear words like "me" and "I" used incorrectly, or sit next to an obnoxious fan at a football game. Invariably I end up back in the arms of pride.

The times I have spent with bitterness and selfishness have been as dark and deep as a pit. I've tried to convince myself that I can't relate to selfishness because I enjoy giving gifts and other pleasantries to people. But selfishness convinces me I want presents, too, and when I think about it too much, selfishness turns to greed. That's when bitterness sets in. Hand-in-hand, the three of us slide down the slippery dark hole.

Of all my metaphorical husbands, shame is the most persistent one, like the man Jesus told the love-lost woman she was still living with. Like a jealous boyfriend, shame will just not let go, constantly reminding me of my weaknesses and unholiness to a God Who calls me to be as holy as He is. Shame plagues me when I make poor decisions, scorn a stranger, or skip church. Never quiet, especially at night when I try to sleep, shame hisses reminders of failures and blunders from the past. Shame sneers, "Tomorrow is going to be just as bad. You are a loser."

Except, tomorrow is today, and I am at the well reading about the Samaritan woman. Here in the fourth chapter of John, Jesus gives us His water so we can live free again. His Love is a thundering waterfall crashing through our bondages, washing away the stigma of our sins.

This is what you and I, along with the Samaritan woman at the well, have needed all along—the Love of Jesus! He offers Living Water and drenches us in His Love.

The story of the Samaritan woman is a lifeline to those of us who think our sins are hidden away in the corners where we hide them. Jesus sees every one of those faults, and He loves us despite ourselves. No matter how many "husbands," or sins, we have, if we'll just ask Him, He'll pluck us out of those corners and throw us back into the world dripping with love.

Drink up the water Jesus pours and live!

For with You is the fountain of life . . . (Psalm 36:9)

DON'T THROW IN THE TOWEL

S atan would have had me throw in the towel. I needed spiritual therapy, possibly CPR.

My spirit was sprained, almost broken. I felt injured, offended, and rejected. My worship had lost its power, my prayers were weak, and my faith was faltering. The hope I inhaled was hot, and instead of praising God, I choked on my words.

On the day of Pentecost, I stood upright when I should have been on the ground; I spoke sharp when I should have babbled joyfully. I was stone cold when I should have been drenched in tears of Living Water. Why couldn't I hear the voice of God? Where was the Holy Spirit when I needed Him? Was I so far out in the wilderness that He couldn't find me? The devil would have liked me to think so.

Satan hissed, "You don't belong. Go back behind your nice, quiet walls. You don't fit in here."

That was where I was in the spiritual realm, and in the physical world, it was how I felt during a particular week when I had to go back to physical therapy. Satan had his grip on me there, too.

Have you been in a battle on uneven ground, so low the darkness pressed hard against you, and you could only hear the cackling voices of the enemy on all sides?

Sometimes, we forget where the *real* battle is being fought.

For our struggle is not against flesh and blood, but against
the rulers, against the authorities, against the powers of this
dark world, and against the spiritual forces of evil
in the heavenly realms. (Ephesians 6:12, NIV)

I had once been agile, mobile, and energetic and had not needed therapy to keep fit or keep up. All body parts worked well as I reveled in my ability to run, jump, and dance, preaching the mantra of fitness: "No pain, no gain!" I thought I was invincible.

When I was diagnosed with rheumatoid arthritis, Satan sneered at the cruel joke. My body caved in and my faith faltered. What was once strong grew weak, what used to stretch became brittle, what had moved so easily broke down, and what kept me fit now hurt. It was all pain. I often got mad at God. He loved me through it, nevertheless. I felt war-weary with life, but my battle was being fought in Heaven.

Satan had a heyday with me in physical therapy. At one time or another, I scooted around in a wheelchair, wore therapeutic boots, and had my fingers splayed in splints. Meanwhile, Satan cunningly used pride and self-pity as very effective weapons.

Most physical therapists have bodies that advertise, "I read life's warning signs. What about you?" and are extremely knowledgeable about how well properly working anatomy is supposed to function. Their job is to teach the malfunctioning bones, joints, and tissues to work again—as well as possible—but not to mend broken hearts or feelings that got hurt.

I wanted to be strong again; the physical therapists wanted to help me manage with my weakness. Satan wanted me to give up. But God knew the truth. I was made perfect in His image—perhaps not whole . . . but holy. Physically and spiritually, I am His Beloved. He would never leave me out in the wilderness.

God reminded me of this during one of those dull, repetitive PT sessions when the exercises were mildly aggravating and excruciatingly boring. A retired doctor, who had treated me for several years after I had been diagnosed with RA, showed up in the clinic. We recognized each other and, hoping he would not notice my advanced deformities, I started to pull away. He smiled, disarming me with the warmth of friendship, and we chatted about our families. After a few minutes, he patted my crooked hand and said, "You know, it was patients like you who made my job as a physician worth it all!" Taking in a deep breath of fresh air, I smiled back.

Just like that, God defeated Satan's attack on me. In fact, before I even knew I needed it, He had already won the battle years before by giving me grace when I had been so sick. The doctor's kind words reminded me that I have always been God's reflection, never His broken toy or failing superstar.

The truth of who we are in God is not in how we perform, how our bodies look or function, or how we worship in church. We are here to carry out Christ's mission to establish the Kingdom of God on Earth.

> And who knows whether you have not come to the kingdom
> for such a time as this? (Esther 4:14b)

We may not be in stellar shape physically or spiritually, do things as well as we once had (or the way other people do), but we are in perfect form this moment for whatever it is God is calling us to do. When the battles rage in Satan's garb of strongholds, we always have the weapons to defeat them. Dressed in the full armor of God, our true identity is in Him, and the victory is ours. The sides were chosen long ago, and our battle has been won.

Take *that*, Satan.

> The weapons we fight with are not the weapons of the world.
> On the contrary, they have divine power to demolish strongholds.
> (2 Corinthians 10:4, NIV)

FROM GUILT TO GRACE

If anyone thirsts, let him come to Me and drink. He who believes in Me, as the Scripture has said, out of his heart will flow rivers of living water. (John 7:38, NKJV)

Wrestling with the call to repentance, I've spent a lot of time lamenting my sins. Wrongdoing and wrong-thinking became neon signs, blinking relentlessly in my head. At one point the list had grown so long I decided to record them in case I'd forget and commit one (or several) all over again. Finally, I organized them into an outline to document cause and effect and hopefully stop the progression.

A proud and haughty (wo)man—"Scoffer" is her name; (S)he acts with arrogant pride. (Proverbs 21:24, adjustments mine)

The pattern of my sin was alarming, taking me down the slippery slope of self-condemnation. I reminded myself that my sins were not violent, gross, or against the law—God's or man's. However, all of my so-called mild sins had combined to make my real sin blaringly apparent: pride.

By pride comes nothing but strife. (Proverbs 13:10, NKJV)

As I attempted to practice a "life of repentance," I found myself repenting my thoughts, actions, choices, and motives. In case my pride had deceived me, I made a concerted effort to forgive anyone I could think of who had offended me from my past—my cousin for ogling like the Boogey Man from behind a bush, my mother for telling me I had no rhythm (I've since learned all humans learn rhythm from their mother's heartbeat), and even the nurse for yanking my leg when I broke my hip. There were so many more to forgive, which was the easy part. These people had mistreated me in some way long ago, and I sincerely forgave them. When I did, my heart didn't hurt as much.

I struggle more with people who irritate me almost every day, like the drivers who cut me off, the vet who shaved my Schnauzer's curls, the contractor who put the light switch in the wrong place, and people who interrupt me. I don't like being offended or contradicted. My pride is easily irritated. It is so hard to forgive *everybody* all the time, especially myself. To dig my pit deeper, this is the Lenten season when I should identify with Christ's suffering, not whining about mine. Guilt hangs over me like too much hairspray, leaving me stiff and crusty. Like my hair, I look "in place" on the outside, but underneath, I need a good scrubbing.

Finally, after I made a sarcastic remark—albeit witty—pertaining to too many cooks in the kitchen, rather than expressing gratitude to those trying to help, I crumbled. Surrendering to God, I confessed my inability to change. Would God receive the plea of a constant sinner with a critical attitude and quick tongue? In this sorry state, I asked Him for forgiveness.

For Godly sorrow produces repentance leading to salvation, not to be regretted; but the sorrow of the world produces death. (2 Corinthians 7:10)

Like the fragrance of fresh flowers, grace permeated my soul. Here was the assurance I had needed. My confession of being unable to change on my own and my desire to repent were all God asked of me. In return, if I would just lean on Him, He would do through me what I could not do without Him.

If we confess our sins, He is faithful and just to forgive us our sins and to cleanse us from all unrighteousness. (1 John 1:19)

Soon after, during a healing service at church, two young men of God held my hands as I wept and they prayed words of new joy, broken walls, and dancing like David over me. Their vibrant, passionate worship was grace rejuvenating me as they prayed the resurrecting Presence of God into my life.

The repented have what I want—"an abundance of grace and the gift of righteousness" (Romans 5:17); they are right with God, and they know it! The experience of healing is deep in their faith and so crucial to our restoration.

> But if we walk in the light as He is in the light, we have fellowship
> with one another, and the blood of Jesus Christ His Son
> cleanses us from all sin. (1 John 1:7)

This is God meeting us at our point of need in the Person of Jesus Christ and in the body of Christ—our Church.

> And of His fullness we have all received, and grace for grace.
> For the Law was given through Moses, but grace and truth came
> through Jesus Christ. (John 1:16–17)

Repentance opens the door to grace, and by grace, we are healed of our iniquities and given new life. God's grace is not just a bouquet; it is a whole field vibrant with flowers growing as far as the eye can see. What a beautiful place to heal and live abundantly, now and forever!

> I am the light of the world. He who follows me shall not walk
> in darkness but have the light of life. (John 8:12)

SEPARATED

Lately, I have had a problem with sin. Being involved in a Bible study, deep into the Book of Leviticus, hasn't helped either. It isn't that I have been sinning any more than usual (at least I hope not); it's just that there is no escape from sin. I am doomed before the sun comes up.

"You are a sinner! You are not welcome in the community, let alone the Kingdom of God!" Condemnation presses down on my head like a street sewage cover. How will I make my way out of my stench?

Prayer, long talks with my grandson, and a message given by my pastor led me to the red ribbon—the lifeline, so to speak. If you have struggled with questions that have made you feel condemned, let me share in the hopes of changing your perspective, too.

My thoughts: Because I sin, am I in a constant state of condemnation?

My prayer: Show me the hope!

My grandson's counsel: "Sin is absolute demolition. Think BB gun at a plate of glass. Shattered."

My pastor's message: "Unless we are unified in Christ's love, our church is not His Church."

Condemnation puts a noose around our necks and yanks us straight out of the presence of God and everything good He wants to give us. Separated from God, we become disoriented and weak. This is what the beast of condemnation does—presses down, squeezes in, and diminishes hope. Harming our ego, it separates us from the truth, productivity, and worst of all, dismantles unity. Before long, the lies take over, offense chokes the Spirit, and the sinning begins.

When I read Leviticus and saw the word "sin" in a thousand places, I wondered how the Israelites ever had any hope at all. I worried about myself, too. What about my sin nature? God had been adamant about the transgressions of those naughty people. They had to be purified from every sin they committed or even thought of committing. He detailed sacrifice after bloody sacrifice to ensure their penitent obedience.

All of those Laws directed toward sin were designed to cleanse an unholy people to make them holy for a Holy God. God loved His children with such vengeance that He demanded the blood of unblemished animals for their sins.

For the life of the flesh is the blood, and I have given it for you on the altar to make atonement for your souls . . . (Leviticus 17:11)

But the Israelites kept sinning. It was not a good time for livestock.

Is it that sin is nefarious and condemnation cancerous? Has God ever become tired of chasing our sinful backsides? Probably, but His wrath against sin has never wavered in His pursuit of every soul. Why? Because God knows the consequence of sin is death and eternal separation from Him (Romans 6:23). He loves us too much for that.

When we condemn ourselves, other persons, or groups of people, we immediately disconnect from the holiness of God. We become distracted and disturbed by the weird, nasty business of the world around us. We feel unbalanced, estranged, and insecure. Rather than feeling freed and fulfilled, loved, and encouraged, we become stymied and offended by what others do differently, such as speaking in a foreign language, dressing inappropriately, eating too much or not enough, chewing too loudly, or parking in the wrong spot. Then, we think what others must be saying about us is distorted, unfair, and downright outrageous.

Condemnation makes us the victim of whomever we suspect or of ourselves. Sometimes, it even seems God is the attacker. Condemnation is a conspiracy and the devil's work. It builds walls and divides us.

As for You, O Lord, You will not restrain Your mercy from me. Your steadfast love and faithfulness will forever preserve me! For evils have encompassed me beyond number; my iniquities have overtaken me, and I cannot see; they are more than the hairs on my head, my heart fails me. (Psalm 40:11–12)

We do not have to sink into a manhole or scream for deliverance from sin's condemnation. We do not have to slaughter our pets, dress for dozens of ceremonial festivals, tear out our hair, wear sackcloth, or ride a wretched goat outside the neighborhood. When we believe what God revealed to us through the cross and confess our sins, we are forgiven. Jesus Christ sacrificed His life to atone for our sins—once and for all. This is the gift of grace we are given through faith, not because of how much we regret our sins or how sad we are because we know we will fail again tomorrow (or in five minutes). But because of the cross, we are no longer condemned. We are separated from sin but are united with God. We are one!

We just have to hold out our dirty, crooked hands, and He will grab on tight. In His mysterious and miraculous way, God takes the broken and victimized spirit within us and creates a whole new person, one who is "becoming holy as I am Holy." (1 Peter 1:16)

But you are a chosen race, a royal priesthood, a holy nation, a people for His own possession, that you may proclaim the excellences of Him who called you out of darkness into His marvelous light. (1 Peter 2:9, NIV)

LESSONS FROM A BALLERINA

I have had the pleasure of attending our granddaughter's ballet recitals for twelve consecutive years. She danced in three different ensembles this past Saturday—two ballets and one jazz piece. Although Josselyn was one of many lovely and accomplished dancers, her radiance from the stage not only delighted me but struck me with a lesson I will not forget. Some lessons are harder for us to learn than others. God has a way of bringing them back around again.

As Christians, don't we dream to be like Jesus? We hear His call to be holy, loving, humble, and selfless. We want to be His very best servants, so we can feed His sheep and bring His love to the lost and hurting people around us. Our vision is to be Christ-like; our frustration is that it doesn't happen overnight, in a month, or even over a decade. Disappointed in our efforts, many of us turn from Christ's reality to believe instead in our failed performances.

Josselyn showed me that to be a dancer, you have to believe you are a dancer and you have to dance like one every single day, even when you are tired or make mistakes. For a dozen years, she went to hundreds of practices and strenuous training classes that evolved, requiring longer and longer hours, to which she lugged her ballet shoes and leotards in bags with her books and homework after school. Often, she didn't get home until after ten o'clock at night, with no time for dinner. She collapsed in bed and awoke most mornings with a smile of anticipation for the next practice. Every new day was an opportunity to realize her dream. Josselyn has lived her dream like I have wanted to live for Christ. This is the revelation my fourteen-year-old ballerina imparted to me.

If we have a passion for Jesus, why is it such a struggle to serve and obey Him consistently? Why can't we love others as He did? Why is it so hard to be a Christian sometimes? Perhaps, in our desire to be perfect, we use others as our role models rather than Him, or we try to measure up to our church community rather than Christ Himself. I confess at times I exhaust myself by trying to act like a Christian rather than just be one. I forget what I believe and, instead of being joyful, I mope.

Jesus loved people, but He did not try to be like them. He was completely comfortable in His skin as He lived out His Father's vision of love for mankind. This was His call as the Son of Man—His belief. If we want to be like Jesus, we must spend time with Him, reading His words, learning His ways, and believing what He says about us: "Whoever believes in Me will also do the works that I do; and greater works than these will he do . . ." (John 14:12) Only then can we put His truths into practice.

I have watched my granddaughter twirl, tiptoe, plié, and sail across dozens of stages in tutus, flouncy dresses, and long, flowing gowns. In every performance, her hazel eyes blazed with joy, her head held high, and her arms reaching more gracefully each year. Her love for ballet has been palpable, whether she dances in the front or very back of the stage. Her platform has been her commitment to the dream God gave her, and she surrenders it back to Him in worship every time she dances.

Through my granddaughter, I have seen passion take form. For years, we watched her emerge, giggling and gangly, upward toward her dream of becoming a ballerina. Now, with aplomb, she is strong and confident upon satin-lined pointe shoes, reaching elegantly toward heaven with nimble fingertips. When she smiles, she fills the auditorium with her bright joy. The dream she believed in has always been true—she *is* a ballerina.

When we believe in Jesus, how can we doubt ourselves? We don't need practice to perform; we need Him. It is with Jesus Christ alone that we can be right with God and perfect in His eyes. As the Apostle Paul declared, "In Him we live, and move, and have our being." (Acts 17:28)

Believe that who you are in Christ is true, and dance!

> *You've gotta dance like there's nobody watching,*
> *Love like you'll never be hurt,*
> *Sing like nobody's listening,*
> *And live like it's heaven on earth.*
> —W.W. Purkey

DECORATE YOUR LIFE WITH JESUS

The day after Christmas can be bittersweet. While it comes with merry memories and gifts galore, it also leaves in its wake celebration clutter and an uncomfortably loud quiet.

The emotions of the Christmas season run the gamut of awe, wonder, and excitement for those surrounded by friends, family, and church. It can be a time of sadness and loneliness for people away from home or who have lost loved ones. Either way, the holidays carry with them an expectation. The magic of Christmas dovetails with the holiness of Advent, offering all who reach for it a promise of something new, something better. When the day is done, the tree lights are turned off, the candles are blown out, the dishes have been cleaned, and the last "Merry Christmas" said, a collective sigh, "Where do we go from here?" circles through the air. For many of us, fear slithers under the door the day after Christmas, a time when the reality of the coming year emerges. We want to keep Christmas all year round.

Just a week into December my daughter lamented that after Christmas, there would be no more lights or decorations. Yes, my child, those lights beckon warmth and goodness, but they are decorations and it's time to turn them off.

"We need to keep them up until spring!" she wailed. "The sparkling lights make such a difference on dark winter nights."

My son-in-law made a prophetic suggestion to his distraught wife. "Let's decorate our lives with Jesus this year!"

Yes, Church, let's clean up and pack away our holiday jubilee and find beneath the litter and collections the mantle and cloak passed on to us. It's time to shine bright with Jesus! Let us remember we are not being saved; we are saved. We are not becoming a church; we are the Church!

Paul wrote explicitly to the Romans about how to behave like Christians, describing perfectly how to decorate our lives with Jesus.

> Love from the center of who you are . . .
> Don't burn out; keep yourselves fueled and aflame.
> Bless your enemies; no cursing under your breath.
> Laugh with your happy friends when they're happy;
> share tears when they're down.
> Get along with each other; don't be stuck up.
> Make friends with nobodies: don't be the great somebody.
> Discover beauty in everyone.
> Don't let evil get the best of you;
> get the best of evil by doing good.
> (Romans 12:9,11,14–16,17,21, MSG)

"Get out of bed and get dressed!" is The Message's paraphrase from Romans 13. "Don't loiter and linger, waiting until the very last minute. Dress yourselves in Christ and be up and about!

In a dark world overshadowed by sin's tragedies, we are Christ's Light and we must shine brightly. Our darkness seems to be a reality, but it is not impenetrable.

During the days of Advent, I took time early in the early morning to be present with God and let Him unwrap His gifts in me. One of the things He brought to me was a book I'd read years ago, *The Day Christ Was Born* by Jim Bishop. I was so blessed by this reverent reconstruction of our most joyously celebrated event. While reading it, I believe the Holy Spirit led me to a realization inclusive of the idea of being dressed in Christ.

Before Jesus was born, people who wanted to be in the presence of God built altars to offer sacrifices of blood for gratitude or repentance preceding or following a significant supernatural event.

Noah built an altar of thanksgiving and celebration when he finally reached land after spending 150 days on a self-built ark with his wife, children, in-laws, and thousands of animals (Genesis 8:20)

Abram (later named Abraham) built an altar to worship God after it was promised that he and his descendants would live and be blessed In Canaan (Genesis 12:7).

Moses built an altar to honor God after he received the Word of the Lord and wrote the Book of the Covenant (Exodus 24:4).

Elijah repaired and built up the altar on Mount Carmel to prove the superiority of God over Baal (1 Kings 18:30).

David proclaimed an altar of thanksgiving in Psalm 26 and of repentance in Psalm 51.

However, when Jesus the Son of God was born, Mary and Joseph celebrated this greatest event on Earth quietly and peacefully in a stable. The shepherds, called by angels hovering in the night sky over their pastures, visited the holy baby and left with joy and hope in their hearts, for they had seen with their own eyes the promised Messiah. They needed no altar; they had been with God. The Magi who followed the Eastern star to Bethlehem rose from their knees where they had worshipped the newborn King and went back to their lands, not to build an altar, but to deliver the Good News about the new baby lying in a manger.

When it came time to leave, Mary and Joseph exited the stable where they had reposed in prayerful celebration with their holy newborn. Their altar was their love for their baby and the divine mission of His Life. The Christ child was wrapped in His mother's arms as He went with His parents into the world. In a sense, Mary was decorated with Jesus. So we are to be.

The new altar for mankind is the cross of Christ (Hebrews 13:10). Jesus came into this crazy, wretched world to be our sacrifice so that we can be in the presence of God through our faith alone. No condemnation, no punishment, no wood nor stone, and no animals, just forgiveness and love.

. . . how much more shall the blood of Christ, who through
the eternal Spirit offered Himself without spot to God,
cleanse your conscience from dead works to serve the living God?
(Hebrews 9:14)

How do we keep the true Light of Christmas all year long? My wise son-in-law said it best: "Decorate your life with Jesus!"

Begin on the inside, for "yours is the temple of the Holy Spirit" (1 Corinthians 6:19). Worship Him from the altar of your heart and take His Light out into the world. Every day of the year.

ARE YOU READY?

Jesus Christ's promised return to earth can be a daunting thought for some of us. When I saw the movie, *Secretariat*, and the horse reared up from behind his gates, exploding with fury and victory, I thought, "Yep. That's how it's going to be when Jesus comes back!"

Maybe it will be like that when He comes in the clouds. If I am here, I want to be dressed and ready! Recently, I reflected on a few of my life experiences and decided that to be ready for Jesus, I needed to have hope and faith . . . and to shave my legs. I want to be ready.

My husband and I had the opportunity to go to Florida in our RV for the month of March. I actually felt guilty when we left behind sleet, snow, and dreary, cold and drove south to meet with blue water, palm trees, and bright skies for the rest of the winter. I was blessed and I knew it.

Our days in Florida were warm and bright, but it was on our return home that I sensed the miracle of the Easter season. As we traveled north toward Virginia, a panorama of promise floated toward me, and I felt as if I was on the edge of a miracle. The evidence of spring was everywhere! Daffodils waved, cherry trees bloomed, white and pink dogwoods ruffled.

I remembered how bleak and cold everything was when we had left our home in the winter and thought of Jesus' last weeks on earth when the atmosphere was tense, threatening, and confusing to all who were with Him—of their shattered hope when He was crucified. Then Jesus returned in glory after being with His

Father in Heaven, bringing new life and hope to the world. He came with this promise, "I will come again and will take you to myself, and where I am you may be also." (John 14: 3)

While we were in Florida, we took a couple of days to drive to Orlando to visit our daughter's family while they were on vacation at Disney World. Our six-year-old granddaughter, Meredith's, parents did not tell her that we would be at the Crystal Palace to join them for dinner with Winnie the Pooh. Their intent was not only to surprise her but also to help to contain her excitement that had been nearly out of control since the day they arrived.

As my husband and I waited by the Palace, we tried to stay behind the crowd so when Meredith and her family arrived, we could watch her excitement in its natural state. It was easy to spot the blonde pigtails, whirling in the air, as they approached. As we expected, our granddaughter was hopping, twirling, and leaping in front of her sister's stroller, obviously unable to stifle her joy. It was The Magic Kingdom, after all!

We could see her head turn to us and the breath she sucked in as she processed whom she saw. Suddenly, all of her flailing movements aligned in the same direction, and her body crashed into mine. Her eyes were bright with joy and sparkling adoration as she jumped up and down with me still in her grip.

"I knew you would come! I *knew* you would be here!" It seems we did not surprise our granddaughter at all. She had faith that we would show up at The Magic Kingdom. She just *knew*.

That's how we should be when Jesus comes back! We should have the pure, unplugged faith of a child and go running, hobbling, or wheeling into his open arms!

> Let the children come to me and do not hinder them,
> for to such belongs the kingdom of God. (Luke 18:16)

We should begin every day with joy as we serve the Kingdom of God on earth in anticipation of the Messiah's return. Even if some days are difficult, messy, and exhausting, and we don't even feel like shaving, we must be ready for Jesus. If we believe His words, "You also must be ready, for the Son of Man is coming at an hour you do not expect" (Luke 12:51), we must be diligent in all we are called to do so that He finds us faithful.

As recorded in the Gospel of Luke, Jesus admonished His followers to wait for Him. Over two thousand years later, Christians are still waiting. Sometimes the wait is arduous and painful, and waiting for God's better world to come seems unfair and way overdue. The Lord is with us, and He promises to help us as we wait and believe.

He gives us hope, as in the arrival of spring. "Behold, I am making all things new." (Revelation 21:5)

He gives us faith, as our grandchild had, to believe in something we know but cannot fathom. "Now faith is the assurance of things hoped for, the conviction of things not seen." (Hebrews 11:1)

We are to live out our beliefs in our daily lives. Through His own example, Jesus showed us exactly how we are to wait for Him so that we will be transformed to be like Him in compassion and universal love, to receive Heaven's greatest reward—life in eternity with His Father.

Not everyone who says to me, "Lord, Lord," will enter the kingdom of heaven, but the one who does the will of my Father who is in heaven.
(Luke 7:21)

Hope. Faith. Belief. He's coming! Are you ready?

HOPE FOR A SLINKY

May the God of hope fill you with all joy . . . (Romans 15:13)

The story of the paralyzed man Jesus healed, as told in the Gospels of Mark and Luke, is a pain therapist's clinical dream come true. But for those who know Jesus Christ, the Son of God, it is the proof of a miracle and of His grace.

"This is how our autonomic systems should operate. Our brain and nerves work harmoniously together, keeping our breathing and heart rate regulated."

The slinky vacillated in smooth silver arcs, up and down, over and back, as my pain therapist demonstrated the human nervous system. The toy's rhythmic clinking was mesmerizing. I could watch those sheared ovals play all day. If only life was like that.

Suddenly the therapist's hands pumped up and down, causing the slinky to lose its consistent motion, making erratic coils and arcing swirls. The clinking melody changed to frantic slapping.

"When startled," the therapist continued, "our hearts pound, our breathing speeds up, our muscles tense, and our bodies prepare for fight or flight. When the alarm has passed, the body relaxes, our heart rate slows down, and we give a big sigh of relief."

Unexpected and incomprehensible interruptions to our balanced lives cause our slinkies, or nervous systems, to go awry. This is when we feel tense, anxious, agitated, and plain crazy. Daily life is cluttered with an ever-rising scale of chaos.

"That's when the slinky slumps." The coils in the doctor's slackened hands fell toward the floor. Have you ever felt like a slumping slinky? That's when it's time to get a push.

God created us with an expertly trained army of nerves. But what if the fear is traumatic and ongoing? The doctor clamped the sagging slinky hard between his hands to demonstrate what stress-trauma physicians have recognized as a more serious effect of fear, termed appropriately "freeze." While the fight or flight response is about survival and is activated when we believe there's a chance to escape, the freeze response gets activated when there is no hope. Hunters recognize this "deer in headlights" reaction. Many animals freeze when they sense predators. Their autonomic system shuts down, and they fall into a near-death state, which often fools the attacker who is not interested in dead meat. When the danger is gone, the animal's nerves reactivate, and almost miraculously, it comes "back to life," able to escape.

Humans also become "paralyzed" with fear. Fear is evil and the curse of the world. We are afraid of sickness, tragedy, poverty, loneliness, and especially death. Fear destroys hope. When there appears to be no hope of rescue, we perceive we are overcome and we "freeze."

In Capernaum, where Jesus was teaching, there was a man so paralyzed he couldn't move unless someone was willing to carry him. We aren't told how the man became paralyzed or how long he had suffered with his disability—it possibly could have been his whole life. It appeared this pathetic creature had been doomed to his death-like existence forever. He had no hope.

Hope deferred makes the heart sick. (Proverbs 13:12)

The paralytic must have had a compliant nature, for he let others care for him. Surely, he had known about Jesus because his devoted friends had so much faith that they relieved his fear and picked up his mat. When they hauled the paralyzed man to the roof of a home and lowered him, Jesus stopped His teaching and went to them.

The four guys had hope. They knew if they could just carry their friend to Jesus, he would be healed. What look of Holy Love did those men see in Jesus' eyes when He acknowledged their faith? Oh! That we in our faith would also sense such love as those men must have seen!

Close your eyes and try to visualize how Jesus gazed into the eyes of the weary, wasted man on the tarp between his friends. What could the Son of Man impart to one so downcast, depressed, and deformed?

First, He called him "son." Knowing the desperate man had to trust Him, Jesus welcomed him into His family, the Kingdom of God.

Jesus then gave the paralytic what he had lost long ago: eternal hope. "Your sins are healed." The prisoner of paralysis was set free from his past. (Matthew 9:5)

The chains of paralysis broke, the "freeze" melted, and the man who had spent his days flat on a mat was free to run, dance, and rejoice! His fear of lifelong entrapment was replaced by the Love that "casts out fear."

This, too, is our hope. Fear of abandonment, punishment, blame, and shame compresses our slinky and keeps us stuck to our mats. Run, don't walk, to the cross, where Jesus is waiting. If you are pressed down and unable to move, reach out, call for help. You, too, have friends who will carry you to Jesus to be healed.

There may be crowds surrounding Him but push through. Jesus is waiting for you!

And the prayer of faith will save the one who is sick, and the Lord will raise him up. And if he has committed sins, he will be forgiven. (James 5:15)

PIMENTOS AND PICKLES

Spiritual confusion is not a bad thing—unless we handle it wrong. Learning to trust God when things go awry reminds me of the story about a man who had partied a little too much and discovered he lost the keys to his car. Under the bright glare of a streetlamp, he crawled on his hands and knees to search for them.

A man walked by and seeing the frustrated party-guy clawing through the grass, asked him what he was looking for.

"My keys! I can't find my car keys!" was the anguished mumble.

Not seeing any car parked near the streetlight where the man groveled on the ground, the passer-by offered to help. "So where is your car?" he asked.

"Somewhere on the next block, across from my buddy's house where I dropped my keys!" retorted the man, pointing down the darkened alley.

"Why are you looking for them here, a block away from your car?"

Disheveled, the unsteady man stood and looked incredulously at the stranger. "Because it's too dark down there. I can see better here under the light!"

Confusion can make us crazy when it seems everything is dark. Spiritual confusion is especially difficult if we try to reason our way out of darkness, arguing with God about the unfairness of it all. When the faith of yesterday flounders with the changes of today, we may question God's wits or whereabouts. How easily we forget His sovereignty and wander from His truths in search of our own solutions.

Season stepping these days, I have been trying to figure out just where God is leading me. Summer is not quite gone and autumn hangs around the corner. My surroundings are still green and lush, the air warm, and the sky sunny and clear. Yet the shadows are lower, the mornings darker, and the birds' songs louder, more urgent. The pools are closed, the streets have grown quiet with the children back at school, and my family seems far away from me. A change has taken place, and I feel like I've lost something. I question God: "Where do I go? What am I doing wrong?"

It seems as if life is playing tricks everywhere I turn, and they aren't funny. I'm too old for this. For example, why don't grocery stores just leave the food in the same place? Why do they keep moving items around so I can't find them where they used to be? I take the time to write out my menus, find my recipes, and list the ingredients. I drive to the same grocery store as always, park the car, choose my basket, sanitize my hands, and shop. It seems every other week, the canned goods are where paper products were, the plastic bags and aluminum foil are on the pasta aisle with coffee, which used to be with the cereal (where it made more sense), and the produce has been moved to the cheese and eggs bins. The change drives me crazy, taking me twice as long to get through my list compared to when I knew exactly where the pimentos and pickles were because they are not where they were.

Don't grocery store managers know I want to find my things where they belong, buy them, and go home to cook? I don't want to be forced to walk around a newly decorated store with elevator music pumping through the sound system, to be coerced into buying organic coffees or locally farmed produce. Like the obstinate Israelites, I want my meat and bread, not some new-fangled manna. Change confuses me; I don't trust it. It leads to temporary darkness.

Some things in my church have changed, too. This is not a good season to revamp my worship program. I want the old routine, the same seat in the pew, the familiar worship songs mixed with a few hymns, an inspirational message, a congregational blessing, and a pleasant drive home. I need the Church to be reliable and restful, a place I can find God in the same place He was the week before . . . and the week before and the week before. Why can't things stay the same?

Spiritual confusion happens when we don't understand what's going on, and we forget to trust God. To be confused is not right or wrong but losing our faith in God's purpose for us is wrong. Even if we feel disoriented and disconnected, we must remember God has a purpose. He has a plan, one allowing us to be right where we are. We may not feel Him with us, but He is present; we may feel lost, but He is protecting us; we may not understand, but the plan is His. Spiritual confusion can only be conquered through obedience. Only by obeying and trusting God while going through change, hardship, and darkness can we ultimately understand what He wants from us. Sometimes, He wants us to just stand firm, and other times, He has something bigger for us which will require us to be active. Our faith must not waver.

Our favorite grocery stores move their products around to better serve their customers by giving variety and a pleasant shopping experience. The seasons of our lives evolve as we learn to trust God's goodness and stay in the center of His will. The changing seasons of nature were created to keep the Earth in balance. The Church comes alive with the spirit of God when we seek His presence over our preferences.

God allows, even designs, change in our lives to confound and uproot us from complacency. Confusion in the midst of change shakes us out of self-reliance and brings us full center to the foot of the cross. There, when we submit our doubts and arguments to Jesus Christ, the Son of God, we find truth and life. (John 14:6). As we trust and obey Him, our darkness is filled with the redeeming light of His purpose, and we come alive again. The Life of God in us is not about the good old days but in the making of all things new!

For the mountains may depart and the hills be removed,
but my steadfast love shall not depart from you . . . (Isaiah 55:10a)

CHAOS AND CREATION

I wonder if I will ever learn.

Day after day I am given opportunities to proclaim the name of Jesus Christ, to express His love, even to share the Gospel with another. I want to be that kind of Christian. The kind who reaches out to others, even strangers, pats them on the shoulder, and says, "God has impressed upon me to tell you Jesus loves you so much," or "May I pray for you?" But no, I let so many sacred opportunities pass me by. What is God going to do with me?

For those of us who love God, every circumstance is sacred. Everything in our lives is designed for our ultimate good in the Kingdom of God.

We know that all things work together for good for those who love God.
(Romans 8:28)

As we muddle through our daily matters, face crises, and climb the long winding stairway of life toward Heaven, the concept of living sacredly and making each minute count can be pretty daunting.

I keep failing, like last week when I ended up in the hospital and was sicker than a dog—not exactly missionary material. I had been retching for twelve hours with a headache that made me wonder if I'd been hit with a bowling ball. I had already been taken to Urgent Care and was getting weaker and sicker by the minute. Did I go to the ER with a halo over my head or even a sweet "Jesus loves you" smile? No, I croaked, "Get me a bed."

I was visiting my pregnant daughter in Northern Virginia so that I could play with my granddaughters and accompany her for an ultrasound appointment. My sudden illness was inconvenient, to say the least. How could I consider it a "sacred circumstance?"

The physicians at the hospital were of different nationalities and cultures, all very skilled and seriously focused on my condition. It was a mission field, of sorts. My doctors were anxious to run tests to determine if I had bacterial or viral meningitis. Meanwhile, they gave my daughter a mask and instructions to "back away."

While the doctors ran tests on me, my three daughters and husband were praying over the phone, pleading for God to intervene, heal me, and give me peace. Normally, I am paralyzed with fear in medical situations and am overly compliant and kind to all the medical staff. This is not because I want to pray with them but because I know my welfare is in their hands, and I want them to like me. My whole family knows only too well my fear of hospitals. While they prayed, I remained almost comatose, not socializing at all.

Did I pray while I was being treated and tested for meningitis? I only remember saying, "Jesus, Jesus," over and over during the spinal tap. But I was not afraid. Nothing about the whole experience frightened me. I felt like I was in a cocoon where nothing from the outside could threaten me on the inside.

As soon as the medicine dripped into my veins from two different IV bags made me feel better, I complimented one doctor on her blouse and politely asked another to refer to needles as "lollipops," which he did. I believe the Holy Spirit had begun to whisper His love into my beleaguered body. I just wish I had told a doctor or nurse that Jesus loves them too.

In spite of the frustrated warnings of the medical staff wanting to keep me in the hospital for more tests, I left the next day, completely well. Every test they had run came back negative; they could find nothing wrong with me. Why stick around?

I wish I had gathered them all together to tell them I believe in prayer and miracles. I did not, however; I went home to play with my granddaughters.

If it is true that God brings us to places, people, and certain conditions for His purposes, how could those two days I had been so sick have meant anything for His Kingdom?

. . . but the Spirit Himself makes intercession. (Romans 8:26)

The most important part of the mystery of sacred circumstances leaves everything completely in the providence of God. We are the channels of His Spirit. We have no idea what He is doing through us wherever we are, but we can take comfort that it is a good thing.

The faces of every one of my doctors and nurses keep passing through my mind clear enough that I am aware of them, as I had been when they were taking care of me. Now I pray for them, face by face. Perhaps this is all God wanted from me.

Intercessory prayer is the most powerful tool in the Kingdom of God. It is how God will reach the entire universe for His glory. We may not be articulate, quick-thinking, or bent toward evangelism, but we can be His channels of love. We must keep our conscious minds open to the Holy Spirit and allow Him to purify our perceptions so that our lives are fertile ground for His saving work.

Two days after I had been released from the hospital I was back again. I found myself in a darkened room with my daughter and her ultrasound tech, washed in the miracle of seeing my grandson swimming and squirming through the aqueous comfort of his little space. *Pump, pump* went his strong heart, round was his belly filled with maternal nourishment, and busy were his stretching limbs. His soft head encased a brain already processing his mother's love. Seeing this nine-ounce miracle man brought me to my knees.

How could I ever question God's plan or sovereignty? He's the One who made light from darkness, brought life from death. The next time I wonder about the sacredness of my circumstances, I hope I will remember, chaos or creation, it is all His.

In the beginning God created heaven and earth. And the earth was without form, and void; and darkness was upon the face of the deep. And the Spirit of God moved upon the waters. And God said, "Let there be light." And there was light. And God saw the light: that it was good. And God divided the light from the darkness. (Genesis 1:1–4)

ARE YOU IN?

Epiphanies sneak up in the strangest ways. A scene from the movie, *Good Will Hunting* flashed neon-bright from the TV a few weeks ago. The movie, starring Matt Damon as "Will," is about a kid, troubled and angry, from an abusive background, who was cursed—or gifted—with a mind of mathematical genius.

Shawn (played by Robin Williams), a psychologist grappling with the loss of his wife, reluctantly agreed to sort through Will's anger. He came to meet the insolent teenager, armed with a pack of folders filled with reports of Will's past and genius. The kid scowled at the psychologist. "Did you read them?"

Shawn tossed the folders on the desk and looked directly at Will, and here is when the lightning flashed all over the screen for me:

"When you tell me your story, then I will be fascinated. I'm in."

For days, that phrase played over and over in my head: "When you tell me your story . . ."

Recently, I decided to read my Bible first in my morning devotions. Usually, my Scripture reading had come after, in reference to, or alongside, a plethora of other readings by wise, well-known, and respected spiritual writers. It disturbed me when a time or two I was able to read and meditate on all my favorite author's perspectives but then time ran out and I had to leave to go about the day, my Bible remaining closed.

The Holy Spirit didn't like that one bit. I was reading reports, reviews, records, and reflections on God, but I did not know God. Like Shawn indicated to Will, I was not "in," because I had not been engaged in God's story.

So I opened my Bible, which is like a giant heaving heart, pulsating with something living, breathing, and, in a deep sense, moving. "What is it, LORD, You want me to know?" His answer was simply, "Me!"

Reflecting on the resounding reply, I thought about how we approach God's Word. Do we read just to get through it? Do we look for promises, search for answers, seek wisdom, prophecy, values, or do we read the Bible to check off the box? Do we ask God what He wants to tell us?

The Bible is God's story of His glory. Since His glory encompasses the personality, character, and revelation of the Almighty, the only way to capture it is by chewing and savoring every Word of His story. What a clever gift from our Father to give us words to reveal His supernatural glory! Words are so small and insignificant when compared to all the attributes of our Almighty Creator, who could have communicated with us in any way He wished—or not at all.

God gave us His Glory tucked within the inspired words of the Old Testament (Psalm 119:89–90). To unfold His reality to the eternal world, He gave us the Living Word (John 1:1) when He brought forth His divine Son, which we read about in the Gospels (1 Corinthians 2:7–12).

My epiphany makes sense now. God was telling me to read His Word, first!

Sometimes, we have to admit to God we have no idea how to grasp His intention within the inspiration of His Word. We must ask for the help of the Holy Spirit to unpack truths we would never understand by ourselves. As we read our Bibles, we can trust God to do exactly as He promised:

. . . from there you will seek the Lord your God and you will find Him, if you search for Him with all your heart and all your soul. (Deuteronomy 4:29)

And then you will be fascinated. You are in!

WHAT ARE YOU THINKING, GOD?

My faith is floundering; my trust is twisted.

But it's not about me. It's all about others—the good, innocent, and faithful. Ultimately, it is about God.

A son serving in South Africa who could not get a flight back to his beloved mother before she died; a husband who, after forty years, lost his first and only love; a mother of babies battling cancer praying for life while her tormented husband fights darkness; a baby girl with no family tossed around by agencies; a son exhausted from endless nights caring for his gravely ill mother, and a young father weakened by a strange disease. All these stories make me feel as if I've been crying forever. Yet, each one of them proclaims their faith, and Jesus is lifted up.

I am ashamed of myself. Where is my grace? Why can't I beam and proclaim, "God is glorified in all of this?" My heart can't take it.

I have more acceptance—dare I say appreciation—these days for Martha's wailing and whining. I like her a lot.

"Where *are* You, Jesus? What are You thinking, letting this tragedy of my brother's death run amuck? I thought you were his friend!" If I had been there, back in the day, waiting for Jesus in my sorrow, I probably would have recommended Martha try another physician's practice.

When I am angry about something, I get busy. My mind, all cluttered with unsaid words and the unnecessary words I said, makes me want to straighten up something. Like a machine growling, I clean, organize, vacuum, weed, and wash the dogs.

Martha, in her fear and frustration, scurried frantically when Jesus came for dinner (John 12:2) after her brother practically died (well he was dead for a while) and the village was all in an uproar over the Man who had healed her brother, the one she was trying to properly entertain. When He arrived, Mary, sweetness and light amid the chaos, got all of Jesus's attention. I get Martha's tantrum.

Like lamenting Martha, the two disciples trying to make their way to the village of Emmaus two days after Jesus' crucifixion, were blinded by their finite understanding. They had just lost their Friend who had become closer than a brother. He was a Teacher who had taught them the truths of God, untangling knots of distorted legalities, and He had gathered them like lost sheep into His fold, where they learned about a new way of life.

These guys would have done anything for Jesus, and they wanted all of the best for Him. Instead, in horror and terror, they had watched this gentle Man beaten, taunted, tortured, and stripped of all dignity. They witnessed the nails, thorns, whiplashes, and blood. Then, He was gone.

They were inconsolable. There was no way they could even comfort one another. Surely, like me in my stupor, they had railed, "*Why?* Why did He let them do that? If He was the Son of God, why didn't He stop them? What was Jesus thinking?"

They were so deep into despair that when Jesus showed up, looking so much better than they could have expected, they yelled at Him, too.

Are you the only visitor to Jerusalem who does not know the things that have happened there in these days? (Luke 24:18)

And they continued ranting at Him of all the events that, unbeknownst to them, He Himself had allowed. Jesus was right in front of them, surrounding them in all the glory He had promised, but they kept crying.

I can relate to that.

Was it not necessary that the Christ should suffer these things
and enter into His glory? (Luke 24:26)

After hearing that our young friend had not been able to make it home to his
mother's bedside in time, I slammed my elbows down on the cold granite counter
in our kitchen, blinked back scalding tears, and wailed "*What* does God think?
That this is all about *Him*?"

Oops.

I've been in a fight with God. The evidence is clear. I've been trying desperately to do "good works," crying the whole time.

Be gracious to me, O Lord, for I am in distress; my eye is wasted
from grief; my soul and my body also. (Psalm 31:9)

I want to make up with Him now. I am only hurting myself. I want to say
to my Father, "I'm so sorry I've let You down. I have not believed in Your power
beyond my own idea of it. I just don't know how to fix things."

I am reminded through the living, breathing, reassuring Word of God that
when Jesus brought the Kingdom of Heaven to earth, His purpose was to "seek
and save the lost." (Luke 19:10) No more, no less, and He died on the cross to
accomplish it.

Even the Son of God would suffer to carry out God's plan. All sacrifice, as
painful, unreasonable, or tragic as it seems, is worth suffering for His Kingdom.

Jesus is still seeking and saving the lost through those who believe in Him,
even me, questioning, quarreling, stomping, and scowling. He knows I'm not in a
fight with His Father, I'm just a little lost. So He is seeking me and He is seeking
you, pulling us back, giving us grace, and whispering, "Your tears are mine. You
must trust Me. I have not betrayed or abandoned my children. My Kingdom is
coming, and I am gathering the Beloved."

Your kingdom come, Your will be done . . . (Matthew 6:10)

YOUR BANNER OVER ME IS LOVE

"That's just weird." My cousin, Tommy, stared at me. We hadn't seen each other since we were kids, and now we sat chatting at my parents' kitchen table, along with his wife, kids, and my three daughters. We had descended upon my parents' home in sunny Florida for Spring Break, neither of us knowing the other would be visiting at the same time.

My husband, Dan, was not with us because he was at sea.

"He flies jets off an aircraft carrier," I explained, "and usually he's deployed for about six months."

My cousin's brows met between his eyes, and he pulled away as if I had a disease.

"So, he goes away for half a year? What do you do while he's gone?"

What kind of a question was that? Miss him. Stay busy.

"Oh! The regular things," I said nonchalantly. "School, softball practice, ballet, and we do things with the other families whose husbands are gone. Of course, I couldn't manage without God!"

I had tried for seven years and failed miserably.

Tommy smiled, "That's right, you military people get your kids' college tuition paid for!" His absurd and incorrect assumption seemed to justify our family's strange lifestyle.

Our lifestyle was not strange, reckless, or clandestine. It was patriotic and sacrificial. That's how we had looked at it. My husband served our country and defended America's freedom. Our separations were a part of the duty.

But they were difficult.

Love never ends. (1 Corinthians 13:8)

I didn't know it, but God was with me when I was twenty and became a Navy wife. Immature and myopic, I had no identity other than my husband's last name. After Flight Training and several exercises at sea, Dan was deployed for six months. Home alone, learning how to be a mother to our first baby, and keeping house for a man far away was beyond my comprehension or stamina. Marriage was nothing like I had expected.

In spite of my fears and despair, I survived, and Dan returned. Six months later, he was gone again.

Where was God when I needed Him? Why hadn't He just busted through the front door, grabbed me by my maternity dress (I was pregnant again), shake His life into me, and holler, "LEAN ON ME!"

Almost five decades later, I see now how the Lord had been there, not grabbing, shaking, or yelling but pouring His love all over me. Unfortunately, I was not looking for Him—I was looking for my husband. While I pined away the days, thinking my heart had been thrown out to sea and nobody in the world even cared, God was protecting my family and me, guiding me into the joys of motherhood, teaching me fiscal responsibility (quite possibly His ultimate challenge), infusing me with courage, and preparing the way for me to be dependent upon Him, rather than desperate for my husband.

Isn't this the way it is when life, the week, or the hour doesn't work out the way we planned? Suddenly, the ground shifts. The electricity goes out, health insurance costs go up, the car breaks down, the kids get the flu or lice, a hair appointment gets canceled, a scab needs a biopsy, the printer quits, or a twelve-month deployment looms ahead. You don't have to be a whiney Navy wife to panic like Peter in the water *after* He took his eyes off of Jesus (Matthew 14:28–33). When the wind changes, we all tend to look for anything but God.

Before I knew Jesus, I loved my husband only. When he was home, I held on to minutes like treasured pearls; when he was gone, I threw away my life in handfuls of months. Since we could not communicate, except for letters every few weeks, I felt separated from all that gave meaning to life.

If we put our devotion on anyone or anything other than God, we put ourselves on shifting sand. There is nothing in life, particularly in people, that can give us what we need to be truly happy and fulfilled. Why? Because "God is Love" (1 John 4:8), and only in His love, Who *is* love, can our needs be perfectly met in every situation, be it crises or celebration.

For I am sure that neither death nor life, nor angels, nor rulers, nor things present to come, nor powers, not height nor depth, nor anything else in all creation, will be able to separate us from the love of God in Christ Jesus our Lord. (Romans 8:38)

When Jesus came into my heart and the Holy Spirit filled me with God's love, I was given a new identity. Besides being a wife, I was a child of God with an endless resource of capabilities offered at a moment's prayer (sometimes before) and a manual with explicit instructions on how to use them, called the Bible.

Our family still had deployments to deal with for another twelve years, some of them more challenging than others, but I was no longer alone and desperate. During our separations, I joined Bible studies, steeped myself in God's Word, and involved our children in Sunday school and vacation Bible study. I also met wise and inspiring Christians who encouraged me and prayed with me for my husband. These were years of growth in faith, hope, and love—the triad of strength for all Christians.

Early in our walk with the Lord and just before another cruise, my husband gave me a plaque to hang next to the bathroom mirror where I would see it at the beginning of each day. Along with our Navy days, the sign is long gone, but its words still ring true, for, though the field changes, the battle for peace in the Love of God rages on: "There ain't nothin' that will come up today that the Lord and me can't handle."

So we have come to know and to believe the love that God has for us.
God is love, and whoever abides in love abides in God,
and God abides in him. (1 John 4:16)

ME AND MY SHADOW

[Read Psalm 91]

There have been times when I've been accused of being afraid of my own shadow. I'll admit I am skittish in unfamiliar places, at night when I hear weird noises, or within a hundred miles of a snake. If my shadow resembles a predator, real or imagined, the accusation fits. I'm scared.

Even in the safest and most pleasant places, my shadow, the shady image of me created by the angle of sunshine or light, goes where I go. My shadow is me and cannot be trusted.

I am capable of going to unsafe places physically, emotionally, and spiritually. My shadow accompanies me wherever I go: too close to a cliff's edge, in ocean water with sharks and currents, to pet stores with puppies and kittens, to a counter where they're selling coconut macaroons, into a store selling merchandise I don't need, beside me as I force open a door God has already shut, and even by the bedside of a friend who is too young to fight cancer. I am in danger of being besieged by fear, temptation, expectation, and doubt.

As Judy Garland crooned in her old ballad, "Me and My Shadow," even in the presence of my shadow, I feel alone and blue.

I need a shadow I can trust.

> He who dwells in the shelter of the Most High
> will abide in the shadow of the Almighty. (Psalm 91:1)

I need the shadow of El Shaddai, my almighty, overpowering, all-sufficient God. But as I journey through my days, seeking God, reading His Word, and worshipping, I cannot see Him with my eyes—no, not even His shadow—for I am *in* His shadow.

> I will say to the Lord, "My refuge and my fortress,
> my God in whom I trust. (Verse 2)

Through the act of trusting God, I am immediately *in* His Shadow. I am not under, beside, or next to it. I am *in* the Shadow of the Almighty.

> For He will deliver you from the snare of the fowler and from the deadly
> pestilence. He will cover you with his pinions, and under His wings you
> will find refuge; His faithfulness is a shield and buckler. (Verses 3–4)

Last week, when my daughter went to Honduras to care for the children in an overcrowded orphanage, she left me with her two little girls to take care of at home, in their own environment. At the orphanage, my daughter worked in the sweltering kitchen, cleaned out filthy storage bins, rode miles of dirt-packed roads in over-crowded buses, taught dozens of fun-starved children games, combed the hair and polished the nails of little girls who had nothing pretty, and rocked motherless babies to sleep. If Leslie had followed her feelings or agenda while serving in Honduras, she probably would have railed against the corrupt system that oppresses and impoverishes thousands of homeless children, refused to ride in unsafe vehicles, wept uncontrollably at the conditions of the orphanage where the exhausted workers strive to manage needs of unloved, undernourished, vastly under-privileged children and master-minded a way to stow several of those children in her suitcase to bring home. But like all missionaries called by God, she did not follow her leading; she followed God's.

> Because (s)he holds fast to me in love, I will deliver h(er); I will protect
> h(er), because (s)he knows my name. (Verse 14)

Leslie was *in* the shadow of the Almighty as she joyfully prepared meals, organized shelves, hugged children, and poured love, blessings, and pure Jesus on every little head. She was being God's heart!

Meanwhile, back at home, I prepared meals, packed lunches, made beds, washed clothes, bussed and met busses, sang songs, taught games, tied bows, and hugged my two little granddaughters while their mommy was away. I was a little skittish about taking over my son-in-law's wife's territory; I was nervous about driving in the D.C. area with precious cargo, and I really did not want to eat dinner at 5:30 to avoid 7:30 meltdowns. But I was not there to follow my desires or schedule. God filled me with unusual energy, extraordinary patience, great ideas, early morning silliness, and the funniest jokes ever as He kept all of us safe and content. He had me *in* His shadow.

For He will command his angels concerning you
to guard you in all your ways. (Verse 11)

There is an old gentleman living in our neighborhood whose house is in sore need of repairs with a yard of weeds and brush, which he tends as he is able. I don't know his name, but over the years, this man and I have become friends. Every time I see him, he looks a little frailer and more weathered, yet he always smiles and has something good to say about God. Last week, when I walked by his house, he stopped, put down his rake, and slowly ambled over. I waited, marveling at the ray of sunlight framing his head.

"How have you been?" I was afraid he would tell me he had been sick.

"Look!" my friend said, rocking back and forth as if his news was too good to hold in. "The world's in bad shape, and they's trouble ever'where. But look! God is good! Tha's all that matters!"

Ah, such good news to a skittish soul like me. There was no tree near the sidewalk, yet it seemed as if the two of us were embraced by a shadow. We chatted for a while as this man of great faith replenished me with joy and hope. Finally, I asked him to give me a Word before I left.

Those eyes of his pierced my soul. "Look!" He rocked. "Breathe! Take a breath an' fill up your lungs! Feel it?" He waited for me to inhale. "Tha's love straight from God. Jus' breathe it in—God!"

With a long life I will satisfy him and show him my salvation. (Verse 16)

Do you seek God? Are looking for Him, wondering where He is? You will not see Him with your eyes. When you trust Him and call out His name, you will be *in* the all-sufficient shadow of the Almighty, and as He did for my daughter, my old friend, and me, He will fill you up!

Breathe in; breathe out. God!

VICTORIOUS OFFENSE

I have been struggling with a messy little word all week. It keeps popping into my mind, conversations, and books I read, and it even invades my thoughts in the middle of the night when I should be sleeping. This word has been like a piece of bubble gum on the bottom of my shoe. Every time I step forward, the gum sticks and catches my shoe, so I have to stop to work it free, only for it to stick again after a few more steps. When I recently heard in a message at church that God would offend us, I knew it was time for me to grapple with this vicious word: *offense*.

I'd first heard the word loud and clear when someone who loves me dearly offered gentle counsel. "Mom," she said, "I think you are being attacked by a spirit of offense."

Who, me? I immediately tried not to be offended. Even though I pulled off a nonchalant response, *Humph*, I felt trapped and exposed. Was I supposed to receive something from God through her advice, and what did a "spirit of offense" mean anyway? Just what was my daughter, a wise and godly woman, trying to tell me?

It is impossible that no offenses come,
but woe to him through whom they do come! (Luke 17:1)

The Greek word for "offend" in this verse comes from *skandalon,* which originally referred to the part of a trap to which bait was attached, so it was

148

the trigger for the snare. We are more familiar with the definition "stumbling block," or that which causes others to sin, which Jesus strongly warned against. Was a spirit of offense causing me to stumble into a trap that caused problems for others? Still adjusting to normally paced days after a month-long battle with back pain, I was grappling with emotional and spiritual issues. I don't want guilt added to my load.

> It would be better for him if a millstone were hung around his neck, and he were thrown into the sea, than that he should offend one of these little ones. (Luke 17:2)

I needed either a boat or a bathing suit! Caught in a mire of bad habits devised by an insidious spirit of offense, I believe God was tending to the problem. I watched for signs of talons on my heart, just in case my daughter had been wrong, and I deserved an apology.

Aha! There it was, clear as chewing gum on my shoe! My pride told me I'd been wrongly accused. Of course, I should feel offended, hurt, angry, sad, bitter, rejected, and plain mean. See where I was going? Pride was selling me off as a victim. Offense can be a deadly tool to one's spirit if used by the devil.

As the days went along, God showed me the lies Satan had been throwing my way.

"You're old and broken. You aren't needed anymore."

"Healing you is not God's priority. You just haven't learned your lesson."

"The kids have grown up; you need to find your own friends."

"It's too late, you'll never become scripturally literate."

"You can't even make mashed potatoes. Grandmothers are supposed to make mashed potatoes *and* chocolate chip cookies."

"You don't belong at the altar. People will laugh."

"Write devotions? Ha! Who do you think you are, Ann Voskamp's grandmother?"

Every time an accusation stuck, I felt myself returning to my comfortable role as "the victim," where I could nurture my offended feelings. Except this time, with God's grace, I stopped the progression of lies and kicked the trap shut.

> But we have this treasure in earthen vessels, that the excellence
> of the power may be of God and not of us. (2 Corinthians 4:7)

I could either stay miserably comfortable as a victim of my hurt feelings or I could open my heart to God's incredible blessings. I realized I was running from them. Why?

God's goodness can seem so overwhelming and new that we are unsettled by such pure, undeserving grace. This is how God offends us. He will make us so uncomfortable with the stewardship of His outpouring that we may feel threatened and sorry for ourselves. We know we are unable to pay Him back. But when God offends, He cleanses, and He "is faithful, who will not allow you to be tempted beyond what you are able." (1 Corinthians 10:13) God will not allow anything to exist within us because we must live by His Power alone.

> For we who live are always delivered to death for Jesus' sake that the life
> of Jesus also may be manifested on our mortal flesh. (2 Corinthians 4:11)

God's offense is life; Satan's offense is death.

Test yourself on this. Does something or someone offend you? Is the enemy convincing you that you have been mistreated, misunderstood, or judged unfairly, and you have a right to feel hurt and angry? Or are you empowered by God's offense, ready to sacrificially lay down all that keeps you from living fully in Him? Are you a victim or victorious? Will you accept the gracious gift of love from your Heavenly Father?

I'm no victim, nor are you. No child of Almighty God can be overtaken by any power or principality. We are free! In Him, we have peace, power, and joy. Our radiance is His radiance!

> For it is God who commanded light to shine out of darkness,
> who has shone in our hearts to give the light of the knowledge
> of the glory of God in the face of Jesus Christ. (2 Corinthians 4:6)

WAKE UP!

Waiting up for someone can be tortuous. Have you ever tried to stay awake by holding your eyes open, channel surfing, and munching cold popcorn until the key finally turns in the door? If you have ever had a teenager or a spouse who worked late, you've waited up!

We know about dangers, temptations, and mishaps of the night, real or imagined, and we want our loved ones home safely. We become anxious when they are later than expected, not because of the broken agreement, but because there is something greater at stake: their lives and welfare.

In the Garden of Gethsemane, the night of Passover, Jesus asked the disciples, His closest friends, to wait up for Him while He went off to pray.

> Then He said to them, "My soul is very sorrowful, even to death, remain here, and watch with me. (Matthew 26:38)

It was a lot to ask the guys. After all, it had been a long day in Jerusalem. They had to hide in a stranger's house to celebrate Passover then Jesus washed everyone's feet and compared their food and wine to his body and blood. He finished the meal by telling them the astounding news that one of them would betray Him and soon, He would be leaving for the kingdom of God. He spoke in riddles! Finally, after the long dinner and heavy conversation, they sang worship songs and went out into the night air for a walk. It appeared they would be able to get some shuteye in the garden when Jesus suddenly wanted everybody to stay awake. Why? Hadn't they celebrated, prayed, and worshipped enough?

One by one the guys nodded off to sleep.

> And He came to the disciples and found them sleeping. And He said to Peter, "So could you not watch with me one hour? Watch and pray that you may not enter into temptation. The spirit indeed is willing, but the flesh is weak." (Matthew 26:40–41)

Jesus knew what was at stake. He needed to know His followers would be faithful. If they had not given in to their exhaustion, they would have seen the human passion of Christ. Instead, their faith gave way to fatigue.

> And again He came and found them sleeping, for their eyes were heavy. (Matthew 26:43)

Like the groggy disciples, we, too, sometimes let our faith fall asleep. Rather than wait up for God, anticipating His intervention, we just hang on, take one day at a time, and stay plugged into Jesus enough to hope we'll get to Heaven by curfew. Meanwhile, daily life drags us down, we are thrown curveballs, and disaster is around the corner. We are too tired, plodding along to see that God has other issues at stake. He needs us to wake up and trust Him.

Today, as I write this, we solemnly remember the anniversary of the horrific events of the 9/11 attacks on America. During the days and weeks in the aftermath of devastation and death, people driven by fear and confusion thronged to churches to pray and seek God. Life as we knew it was forever altered, and we cleaved to the One we knew could save us, or so we hoped. Our faith was strong, our worship passionate, and our courage gleaned from the power and mercy of God. Eventually, as the black dust settled and daily life picked up its familiar rhythm, even with heightened security measures, the faith of God's people swayed to and fro and drifted off to sleep. Meanwhile, wars of retaliation raged in the Middle East where our young men and women have been sent to fight and die for our safety. The enemies have multiplied and are closing in. It seems easier to escape in sleep than to wait up for God, especially when we're scared, discouraged, and have no idea what He's up to.

Remember Habakkuk, the prophet who railed at God for making rash decisions that would destroy Judah? He did not understand why a God of justice would let so much sin abound or why a God of mercy would allow the murderous Babylonians to be His agents of punishment. Wickedness was growing like weeds everywhere. Yet, Habakkuk didn't run away, climb on the couch with a blanket, or nod off to sleep. He stood firm and worshipped vehemently.

What's God going to say to my questions? I'm braced for the worst. I'll climb to the lookout tower and scan the horizon. I'll **wait** to see what God says, how he'll answer my complaint. (Habakkuk 2:1 MSG, emphasis mine)

If only the disciples had stayed awake like that!

God answered Habakkuk loud and clear with orders to write down His exact words. The Almighty told the persistent prophet that He would punish all the wicked people at the right time, but He alone was sovereign, and His timing would be perfect. God had bigger issues at stake then, as now: the faith of His people.

Jubilant in his own renewed faith, Habakkuk wrote for all of us who must stay awake as we wait and trust the Lord our God who is faithful.

I'm singing joyful praise to God. I'm turning cartwheels of joy to my Savior God. (Habakkuk 3:19, MSG)

More than ever, the world needs to see the action of God awake within us! Don't let the daily drudgeries, battles, or world threats lull you into lethargic exhaustion. Jesus is still calling His faithful to stand firm. We must be willing to put aside our cares and have faith in the great purposes of God for His Kingdom.

Habakkuk wasn't sleepwalking; are you?

THE NEIGHBORHOOD OF GOD

Last week was difficult. Election Day was grueling, our football team lost again, I missed an important doctor's appointment, and I had exchanged angry words with a loved one. Not a good week at all, and I let it get to me.

It's times like these when I want to escape to the presence of God but just can't seem to find Him. They are also the days when I am most amazed and humbled by those who often have difficult days, yet are joyful, kind, and patient:

- The vendors at our local mall who always smile from their kiosks and wish me a nice day;
- The cashier who says, "Take your time," while I fumble in my wallet for change;
- The garbage men who stop the truck and jump out to help me carry garden debris;
- The parking lot attendants who give me directions and their phone numbers in case I get lost.

How is it that these people reflect God's love despite pressing circumstances, yet I cannot get my faith together when things don't go as expected? What weighed on my heart and made my mind race with fear? I began to wonder if I even belonged in the Christian family at all. Lost in self-absorption, my attitude clearly did not reflect the fullness of joy in God's presence.

Let us draw near with a true heart in full assurance of faith,
having our hearts sprinkled from an evil conscience and
our bodies washed in pure water. (Hebrews 10:22)

Thanks to Mike, Mr. Rogers, and my pastor, I now understand how easy it is to drift into the wrong spiritual neighborhood.

Mike, the customer service director at a large, busy sandwich café was the first to welcome me home. Pulled in many directions helping customers choose their menu items, overseeing the cooking staff, and wiping down tables, Mike seemed to be everywhere at once. His smile was infectious, his voice boomed, and his eyes sparkled. Mike took the time to sit with us yesterday as my daughter and granddaughters ate our sandwiches, to tell us the history of the restaurant. He also told us his love of training servers in restaurants all over the country to "serve from the heart."

My spirit lifted; I needed to hear more. There, in a busy restaurant, I had found a wise man. I asked Mike a question then sat back to listen.

"What is it in your heart that you give to everyone and want to teach others to give?"

Mike beamed, "I know God! He is everywhere! See the trees? The sky? How can anyone not know God?" Mike's heart was all over his answer as he told us about his church, its members, and their powerful worship service.

"We whoop it up praisin' the Lord! Yes, we do!"

When the four of us left, he stood at the door waving and blowing kisses. We were family! Mike's joy reminded me that we Christians are never alone, left behind, or left out. We are in God's presence together!

By this all will know that you are My disciples,
if you have love for one another. (John 13:35)

Remember Mr. Rogers? In his television neighborhood, everyone was welcome no matter his or her color, size, age, or wardrobe. Dressed in his infamous sweater and sneakers, Mr. Rogers invited us into a world where curiosity, imagination, and uniqueness were celebrated. His viewers were his friends, and each of us could "make each day special, just by being (us)."

Mr. Rogers reminds me God loves me just as I am, even with my doubts, moods, and unrest. He uses me in my wobbly seasoned form, to make a day special for someone else. God's neighborhood is His presence. I don't have to escape to it. I am there!

Where can I go from your Spirit, where can I flee from Your Presence?
(Psalm 139:7)

In his sermon, our pastor told us our spiritual neighborhood is Goshen—the land of "drawing near," located under the shadow of the Almighty, covered by a Mighty Fortress. God's presence is here, and we are all welcome, just as we are, faulty, frail, and failing, because we are friends of the King, and we are forgiven. In Goshen, my neighbors are the Church—the faithful, grateful, joyful people who give to the world and each other, hope, refuge, and family. They are you and me, and we are home!

For this reason I bow my knees to the Father of our Lord Jesus Christ, from whom the whole family in heaven and earth is named. (Ephesians 3:14)

VACATION WORKOUT

Sticking to a fitness program while on vacation is an oxymoron. Think about it: "vacation workout." It's not going to happen. You go away to rest, not run; to play, not exercise; and to indulge in local delicacies, not count carbs.

Staying spiritually fit while on vacation is also hard, but not because it's work. We are lazy and easily distracted. It is easy to throw in the towel, compromise, make excuses, put "the old self" back on again (Colossians 3:9–10), and promise you'll renew when you return.

"I'm on vacation, after all. I deserve a little slack."

Just like a fine-tuned fitness regimen thrown out the window into the balmy air, causing muscles to slack, fat to collect, and goals to dim, our faith can be blown around a bit, too, while we sit in the sun, ski the slopes, or visit late into the night with friends.

You can believe Satan prowls on vacationers. He is more dangerous than the sun on the skin of a vacationer who forgot to apply sunscreen in the tropics.

I made the mistake of thinking my winter stay in Florida was more of a temporary absence than a vacation. With "Snowbird" status, I could enjoy Florida warmth, sunshine, and a tropical lifestyle while keeping—maybe even stepping up—my fitness protocol. I never even considered changes in my spiritual walk. After all, I had taken my Bible, devotionals, and journals with me. My soul, spirit, and mind would stay intact, even though I was away from my church and morning schedules of quiet time. This could even become a sabbatical!

In less than two weeks of sun, fun, and grouper sandwiches, my spiritual fitness was weak and vulnerable while my physical fitness left me under the bus. I had set my goals all wrong, and God, my Personal Eternal Trainer, was all over me. I ended up in bed with injuries and my Bible. It was time to work out God's way.

Though I walk in the midst of trouble; You will revive me . . . (Psalm 138:7)

Decades ago I took up jogging when the word exercise meant nothing to me but a task of short duration for the purpose of learning, not sweating. Three women that I wanted to get to know jogged by my house every morning as I drank my coffee, chomped down huge bowls of Grapenuts because it was a healthy way to begin the day, and read my Bible. Our family had just moved to Key West, where I prayed for new friends and a body that could possibly fit into shorts. The Holy Spirit whispered, "It's time to exercise!" Little did I know the plans God had for me when I bought my first pair of brown waffled Nikes.

Deciding to practice my new sport (first one ever) after the kids were in bed and my husband was preoccupied with TV, I quickly discovered jogging in tropical heat, even at night, to be tough work. Our block was a mile around, and I could only make it, huffing and puffing, to our neighbor's driveway at the bend, before having to quit—or quite possibly die. No matter how hard I tried or how fast I thought I was running, the misery continued for weeks. I could not even run one-quarter of the way around the block.

"Surely, God," I prayed, "there is an easier way to make friends! I could also settle for wearing long flowing skirts."

One night as I labored along my same failed route, I heard the sound of footsteps gaining on me from behind. I could not run any faster, even when I heard my name. My heart jammed in my throat when I recognized my neighbor, a doctor, loping in shorts alongside me.

"What are you doing?" He was obviously concerned. "Are you okay?"

"Running!" I gasped. What did he think I was doing?

"From what?"

"Nothing! I'm just r—uh—nn—ing." Chatting I was *not* going to be doing.

"Well, why don't you slow down?" With this simple advice, a clear message from God, the good doctor glided effortlessly ahead.

So, I tried it, jogging at a pace I could handle. Slow but steady, I allowed for rests along the way. As my body acclimated to the new stress of exercise, I began to eliminate the stops. Within a week, I could jog all the way around the block. A month later, my friends and I ran together regularly while we chatted about faith and our new Bible study.

God is concerned about our spiritual fitness first and then our physical fitness. They go hand-in-hand because He created us to move and serve actively in His kingdom, but if we are not in top spiritual shape, we will do nothing right for Him in the world. His personalized fitness plan is perfect for each of us. His workout produces endurance, perseverance, and hope (Romans 5:4).

Why didn't I remember that lesson when I returned to Florida instead of trying to exercise like a forty-year-old in a seventy-year-old body? Perhaps, if I had not been so proud and positive I could practice spiritual fitness on my own while vacationing, I would have been more in step with God's guidance.

Even during vacation, we must seek God first. No matter how beautiful the scenery, clear the water, or perfect the weather, the One who provided it all waits for our gratitude and demands our obedience (Deuteronomy 5:29). With every glorious sunrise and magnificent sunset, at home or away, we are always in the presence of God. Do not rush ahead, try to be stronger, or make plans without Him.

The Lord God Almighty *is* our vacation!

Your body is a temple of the Holy Spirit, who is in you . . .
(1 Corinthians 6:19)

ACTIVE STILLNESS

Recently, I wrote, "I find life is better when I can move." Being still is also good, but for many of us, it is a really hard thing to do. Being active is more fun, especially if it is done for a purpose.

When God tells us to do something and we act on it, we experience the exhilaration of trusting Him. We let everything go (at least we try to) as we put our circumstances into His hands and move out in His will. It can be a crazy thing trusting God, and usually amazing things happen.

Enemies are picked off with trumpets, people walk through parted seas, and giants are killed with a kid's slingshot. These are biblical examples. You, too, may have had an experience from a time when you moved out in trust.

Trusting and moving in God's will is easier than being still and waiting on Him to tell us what to do. If we want to hear God's voice, we must be quiet enough to listen. If we do hear a voice, how do we know it is God? Many people today announce how God tells us this or that—as if they had a direct line to His cell phone. Others work hard at trying to hear God speak; they just start talking to Him, hoping for a holy conversation. Still others, like me, mistake Him for someone else.

Once, years ago, I was sure I saw Jesus as I sat praying on my dock in Key West, Florida. I was chatting away, thanking the Lord for the beautiful sunrise and the way it glittered on the water beneath me. With my Bible in my lap, I told Him all my plans for the day and implored Him to join me. Suddenly a silhouetted figure appeared in the blinding sunlight in front of me.

"Oh! Jesus!" I jumped up, waving my arms in worship, nearly dropping my Bible in the water. I exclaimed, "I knew You would come!"

"Uh, hi." The return greeting was not as welcoming as I had expected. Then the approaching shadow revealed, not the Lord but my neighbor, coffee cup in hand, who had also come outside to enjoy the peaceful morning. I'm sure he was as surprised as I was by our unexpected encounter, but I bet no one had ever greeted him more joyfully!

What does it take to really see Jesus and hear His voice?

Be still and know that I am God. (Psalm 46:10)

If God seems to evade our prayers, maybe the still quiet place where we are is overcrowded with self-barging in. When we pray and all we are aware of is condemnation, anxiety, doubt, or a long to-do list, those nasty, interrupting voices must be silenced. We need to still our self-awareness and make room for Christ-awareness.

"Ask the Lord to put awareness of Himself in you, and your self-awareness will disappear." Oswald Chambers suggests in his timeless devotional, *My Utmost for His Highest.*

Sometimes God's silences are opportunities for us to truly abide in Him, surrendering all our thoughts and concerns.

I am the vine; you are the branches. If you remain in Me and I in you, you will bear much fruit; apart from Me you can do nothing. (John 15:5)

To actively serve God, we first must remain still and wait for His answer or direction. Silence is God's almighty activity of the Holy Spirit giving understanding and revelation to the one who waits.

If Jesus Christ is bringing you to the understanding that prayer
is for the glorifying of His Father, then He will give you the first sign
of His intimacy—silence.
(Oswald Chambers in *My Utmost for His Highest*)

SECTION III
THE ESSENCE OF PAIN

UNASHAMED

Pain changes the order of things. It strikes, altering our world, violating and upending everything we thought just the second before was normal, balanced, and right. In one instant, the onslaught of pain turns our right living into "*This* is living?"

Pain is an intruder with many masks. It vagrantly attacks us either emotionally or physically. It is especially vicious when it blasts both realms. A flame, a nail, and a hammer can inflict acute pain that brings us to our knees, makes us throw whatever is close enough to grab, and spew awful words. Unexpected, nerve-shattering pain is mind-bending and often makes us forget our manners.

Fear, anger, and grief are pains of another sort, just as debilitating and paralyzing as seeing blood after slicing a finger. New seasons of life can appear terrifying and insurmountable, like sending our firstborn to kindergarten. Adjustment carries with it angst and anguish.

We have all screamed, "Ouch!" kicked a door, and cried buckets of tears about something that hurt our bodies or feelings. Pain is not a respecter of persons; it is so true it hurts. We recover, the bandage comes off, the scab dries, the refrigerator is covered with colorful pictures and bus schedules, and we move on. Life is good again.

Chronic pain is different. This pain doesn't leave footprints; it leaves laundry, settling into nerve fibers and taking up residence in our souls. When unmitigated pain slams our world, staying upright in that world becomes nearly impossible.

Wounded by a fall or a caustic slur, we can run to someone we love. Fickle chronic pain stymies us, making us wonder if we are loved at all. Sometimes, we don't know what hurts more.

Chronic pain seems to go on forever. Blessedly, the episodes come and go. The caveat is that there is no schedule, no warning, so the victim must always be on guard. At times, this calm-to-crises lifestyle creates a *laissez-faire* attitude, and life is great fun while that lasts. It's hard, though, to ward off the familiar sense of dread of what may be just around the corner. We know it will be back.

Christians face a hefty challenge when put to war with pain. We think suffering is our opportunity to show our stuff and are supposed to react to pain with joy.

"A bee just stung me! Praise the Lord!"

Maybe we can pull that off sometimes, but usually, we focus on the sting more than Jesus. The other day, I sliced my thumb with a bread knife and after the bleeding stopped, I thanked God I had not cut off my whole thumb. I hope my belated gratitude counted in heaven.

C.S. Lewis observed thoughtfully in a letter, "It sounds absurd; but I've met so many innocent sufferers who seem to me gladly offering their pain to God in Christ as part of the Atonement, so patient, meek, even so at peace, and so unselfish that we can hardly doubt they are being, as St. Paul says, 'made perfect by suffering.' On the other hand, I meet selfish egoists in whom suffering seems to produce only resentment, hate, blasphemy, and more egoism. They are the real problem."

As witnesses of our faith to the world, we don't want to be a problem, but while enduring long-term chronic pain, our resolve may tremble. When the headache pounds, the grief won't let go, or the backache debilitates, we cry like the psalmist, "All the day I've been stricken and rebuked every morning" (Psalm 73:14), and we wonder desperately where in the world God is. Suffering should bring the best out in us, but I submit, it is *after* the suffering that we see the grace. We endure as best we can, with all the faith weaponry God gives, and when the pain finally lifts, it is how we recover and enter back into the world that the Holy Spirit shines.

I don't suffer well, nor am I the Queen of Pain. When I am afflicted over and over for weeks at a time, the pain brings out the worst in me. I can endure only so much reading my Bible, listening to praise music, and breathing deeply. Every time, it seems, God brings me to the end of my rope, and I start throwing things, blaring rock 'n roll, and hissing.

"ENOUGH!" I scream.

But it is never enough until my thoughts are spent and I give in.

"Okay, Lord. Have it Your way."

Just perhaps, when Peter wrote that we must "abstain from the passions of the flesh, which war against your soul" (1 Peter 2:11), he knew that while in constant suffering, we are weak and those flesh passions which soothe the hurting temporarily are dangerously tempting. We don't want to go there.

We don't go there because, in our weakness, God is with us even if we can't feel His Hand upon our head. Only when the pain is gone can we look back with a sigh of relief and gratitude. This is our witness. We join our family and friends gratefully, tenderly, and humbly, for we have been with God through it all, and we are not ashamed.

> If anyone suffers as a Christian, let him not be ashamed,
> let him glorify God. (1 Peter 4:16)

THE GIFTS IN PAIN

Suffering breaks the heart of God. He weeps as we weep. In our ordeal of affliction, His tears wash over us.

I have felt God's presence in pain's crucible and found His mercy and love for me there. Through the experience of suffering, God has shown me His beautiful essence within it, and I understand that nothing comes at me without His sovereign permission.

While my goal in life has not been to search for the good in affliction, chronic pain wrapping me in a cloak of daggers over the past several decades has warranted me seclusion and time to ask questions. What is it, I've wondered, about our suffering that God allows if everything first comes through His heart of love?

"There is a divine mystery in suffering, a strange and supernatural power in it, which has never been fathomed by human reason," writes L.B. Cowman.

Suffering is a universal event, unwelcomed, unexpected, and usually unplanned. It ruins a day, alters perspectives, and turns nice people into ogres and mean people into sissies. It shatters plans and dreams and threatens to rewrite our stories. The good news is that God is the Author and His story never changes. He is our refuge, fortress, and shelter, and He is faithful, trustworthy, and strong. No matter our pain, our Sovereign God has a better plan for us.

Because you made the LORD your dwelling place . . . no evil shall be
allowed to befall you, no plague shall come near your tent because
he holds fast to me in love, I will deliver him . . . (Psalm 91: 9,14)

During a recent episode of chronic back spasms, I asked God to take me deep into His mystery. Just what is the essence of pain, the golden thread that keeps us holding onto our faith amid despair and loss of heart and soul? Why, in the throes of suffering, do we cry out to God and question His purpose? Our prayers are deep and desperate. We want our Rescuer even more than relief.

I believe pain is a gift because it ultimately brings us closer to God. In His presence, though the pain persists, His glory pours into us so that we experience the supernatural work of the Holy Spirit. It is here that pain becomes a gift.

Pain teaches *Patience*.

Pain beseeches *Adoration*.

Pain offers an *Invitation*.

Pain ushers us into the *Now* of God's Presence.

Yes, Beloved, in pain, we can know that we are not alone. When He suffered and died on the cross, our Savior knew our deepest needs. No matter the agony, our merciful, compassionate, all-powerful Rescuer accompanies us. His trumpet is loud and clear for the Sufferer to hear:

God has not destined [you] for wrath, but to obtain salvation through our Lord Jesus Christ, who died so that whether [you] are awake or asleep [you] might live with Him. (1 Thessalonians 5:9–10)

PAIN TEACHES PRAISE

He inhabits the praises of people. (Psalm 22:3)

When the spasms abated like a retreating monster licking his chops, I lay on the bed, whispering something like, "Jesus. Jesus. Thank You!" The praise was as natural as my breath, and my heart knew Whom to thank.

And Jesus lifted up His eyes and said,
"Father, I thank You that You have heard me." (John 11:41)

I gazed around the bedroom with a fresh appreciation for every familiar object—the dresser with necklaces hanging like tinsel from the lamp, my bedside table stacked with books about inspiration and comfort, and the window where a tree with sun-painted leaves reminded me it was still a summer day. Yet, it seemed I was in a holy place permeated with praise. Yes, God had been with me all along, and He brought me out of the pain into His peace where I could enjoy Him.

Even though I walk through the darkest valley . . .
His rod and staff, they comfort me. (Psalm 23:4)

When pain strikes, it is sometimes too hard to pray, let alone give thanks. "Thanks for what?" I've wondered in the heat of the battle. "What is the good in this, and how can I endure it?"

Shaken and stressed in our suffering we want God's rescue, not God Himself. But He knows what we need, and only in His presence will we get it. There is a particular power in the praise that arises in distress.

Before Jesus called Lazarus from the grave where the man had been dead and bound in corpse cloths for three days, He thanked His Father for hearing Him. In the midst of great sorrow and weeping, Jesus, also moved to weep, praised His Father for listening to Him. I love that Jesus, in His humanness wept as those around him wept. We, too, must know God always hears our cries. Through the Holy Spirit, He pours praise into our souls. This praise was the power of Jesus that drew Lazarus from the grave, and it is given to us as well when we give God praise in our suffering. Our praise reveals the Glory of God.

I believe when we trust God in the crucible of suffering, He peels from our souls all hindrances which keep us from Him. How sweet our trust is to God, for it was the same with His Son all the way to the cross. In return, He lavishes us with the refreshment of Living Water, the peacefulness of grace, and the holy power of praise.

In pain is the gift of Praise.

Bless the Lord, O my soul and all that is within me, bless His holy name! Bless the Lord O my soul, and forget not His benefits, who forgives all your iniquity, who heals all your diseases, who redeems your life from the pit, who crowns you with steadfast love and mercy, who satisfies you with good so that your youth is renewed like the eagle's. (Psalm 103:1–5)

PAIN IMPLORES ADORATION

Loving God when unexpected pain strikes is really hard, like trying to have kind feelings toward the hammer after it hits your thumb, a bee that stings your arm, or hot grease that has splattered in your face. But after a short rage, which you hope Jesus didn't notice, you get over it and go back to your more benevolent self.

Under the long-term vise of chronic pain, loving God is the only way to survive. He is our only hope, and we depend on that because we can.

> The Lord is my rock and my fortress and my deliverer, my God,
> my rock in whom I take refuge, my shield and the horn of my salvation,
> my stronghold. I call upon the Lord who is worthy to be praised
> and I am saved from my enemies. (Psalm 18:1–3)

Thanking God after a long bout of spasms awakened an electric feeling in my soul. There seemed to be something bursting inside me. With my whole exhausted being, I wanted to sing and dance with joy and see God's face, to gaze at Him in adoration. David knew what my words couldn't form:

> I have set the Lord always before me, because He is at my right hand,
> I will not be shaken. You have made known to me the path of life,
> in Your Presence there is fullness of joy, at Your right hand are
> pleasures forevermore. (Psalm 16:8,11)

What I was experiencing after the wrenching episode of spasms was adoration for Almighty God. How could the peace, praise, and joy pulsating through my veins not make me adore my Father in Heaven who had been at my right hand all along?

God uses hardship, suffering, and affliction to show us where true joy can be found. He rescues us so that we will adore Him and know the beauty of His glory. This, too, is another gift from pain, like "honey pouring from a rock" (Psalm 81:16).

In pain is the gift of adoration.

PAIN EXTENDS INVITATION

The broken sufferer lives in solitude much of the time. Pain, emotional or physical, intensifies the loneliness. Yet, I've found, in the throes of spasms or despair, though I am lonely, I want no company.

So much isolation lends itself to depression. The sense of void is a virtual playground for the devil. Myopia, morbidity, and malaise crowd the bed and the head.

Into this tunnel, the Rescuer whispers hope. Even when the pain pounds and the darkness drones on, an invitation to enter a new glory hovers. It is delivered by a host of angelic messengers, which only the sufferer hears. This spiritual rescue is not a delusion; it is a calling—an invitation to visit the Glory of God.

Lying limp on my bed, my head ensconced in pillows, and electrodes burrowing into my war torn back, I've wondered if I'll ever recover. How could I go back to "normal life"?

When the pain wanes, I become calm, movement returns and reality—as I know it—enters my thoughts. At first my spirit lingers. I feel a difference in my soul pain and I sense the presence of God around me. I do not want to join others, resuming my activities: fold laundry, empty the dishwasher, walk my dog, or even take a shower and start over. I do not want to forget that I have been broken.

In his timeless book, *The Wounded Healer*, Henri Nouwen writes, "Perhaps the painful awareness of loneliness is an invitation to transcend our limitations and look beyond the boundaries of our existence."

As Christians committed to serving Christ by ministering to others as He did, we must suffer afflictions that take us away from this world and into the depths of our souls. Here in this crucible, we face our fears, sorrows, and failings. Jesus walks through every cracked door with us and welcomes us as His—saved, comforted, and adored. These are the gifts, dear sufferers, we bring into the world where people in darkness, pain, and loneliness cry out for compassion.

Pain offers an invitation into the courts of the King. Since He uses all things—including afflictions—for good, we can find purpose in our wretched wounding. To be invited into His courts is to be welcomed into the presence of His Son, Jesus Christ, who sits at His right hand. Here mysterious glories are revealed as our senses heighten in awareness of His presence in all things. Our brokenness is beautiful to our suffering Savior.

> Oh how I love Your dwelling place, O Lord of hosts.
> My soul longs, yes faints for Your courts. (Psalm 84:1)

In pain is the gift of an invitation.

PAIN IN THE NOW

Decades of experiencing chronic pain have taught me how to be more patient. Believe me: This was quite a battle because the stabs of spasms were tempests of pain I had never before experienced. Many days, I was rendered a wailing, wild woman. I quickly discovered I was not the Queen of Pain.

I had visions of clutching the bottom of Jesus' robe, like the ailing woman in Luke's Gospel, not with dignity or sweet faith but with clenched teeth and hot tears, begging, "Jesus! Make it go away!"

As the years went on, and I sought medical help, finding no more solution than just temporary relief with mind-numbing pills, I asked others to pray for me and waited as patiently as I could for healing. Through that time, I learned to pray by myself and found comfort in my conversations with God. I tried to be articulate and intentional in my praying, adding Scripture verses I had memorized. I hoped Jesus would hear my voice and touch me. *Heal me.*

I remember the day I told the Lord it was okay if He didn't heal me, and I surrendered my pain to Him. There was nothing I could do on my own to change this unwanted course of my life. I asked Him, instead, to just give me the grace to bear it. In that prayer, I felt withdrawing from me not the pain, but all the anger, disappointment, and bitterness from my soul. The Holy Spirit then breathed deeply and wholly, expanding my heart. I knew there was another way to live with this pain. I would be obedient to my Jesus through it and allow His grace to pour through me.

I thought, "Surely this was His purpose for the pain, and someday, I will please Him in it."

**He made His disciples get into the boat
and go before Him to the other side. (Mark 6:45)**

Sometimes, we have the idea that God is leading us to a particular goal or purpose, which we just have to hold onto until we get to it. We want something new and we want to do well. I have been waiting for healing, pure and simple. In the meantime, I was working on faith, prayer, and obedience. In short, I was trying to earn my healing and accept it gracefully, if it should come.

When the disciples got into their boat and went off to sea, Jesus turned to a mountain where He could go to pray. Meanwhile, the boat headed into stormy waters.

When a storm hits our life, and it seems we are doomed to the winds and raging waters, Jesus is with His Father praying for us. His eyes are not on the tempest and swirling waves. His eyes are on us and He knows our terror and hears our cries.

**When it was almost morning, Jesus came to them,
walking on the surface of the water. (Mark 6:48, paraphrased)**

In our pain, Jesus prays for us, and He comes to us. It all happens in the midst of what appears to be wreckage and disaster. While we are begging for the storm to be over, our Savior is walking in the storm with us. This is what we must see in our times of suffering. Not *when* the storm will subside, but that Jesus Christ is walking with us on those turbulent waters. We do not have to earn His mercy. He is present!

"And He got into the boat with them, and the wind ceased. And they were utterly astounded" (Mark 6;51). Just like that, He, too, is in our boat. God wants us to know His presence in the moment, to see Him walking on the water, *now*.

What relief, freedom, and joy when we fully grasp that the past can no longer pull at our longings nor the future at our disappointments. The Lord is with us *now* and all is well.

"God's purpose is to enable me to see that He can walk on the storms of my life right now," writes Oswald Chambers in *My Utmost for His Highest.*

This is the last acronym of pain: the *N* for NOW. The gift of pain is not what is next or when there is something new, finally. The gift is the knowing that God is with us *now* and in that, only and wholly, can we glorify Him. This is His gift to each of us in all of our suffering, pain, and loss—Jesus is walking in the waters with us.

In pain is the gift of knowing "Immanuel," God with us, now.

PAIN UNINVITED

Pain arrives, uninvited,
unpredictable,
like a clandestine lover.
Wary, I mark time carefully.

In familiar, dreaded spasms
Pain hisses, persistent, ruthless.
I tremble behind
unprotected boundaries

In the fire of Pain's grip,
I am no longer invincible,
every movement is a gift,
each breath ordained.

Pain's jealousy
takes vigilance over my soul,
allowing no other to share my solitude,
or embrace my misery.

Pain scoffs at my desires,
snatches dreams,
smashes hopes, and smothers
yesterday's treasures.

Yet without Pain's cunning cost,
I would be cold,
distracted, lured
by dangers of another sort.

Lying in silent shadows,
my chastened spirit sighs.
Unleashed, Pain seers my heart,
abuses my soul.

Held as Pain's captive,
I am isolated from the living,
and listen desperately
for my Redeemer.

Hope reigns white light,
Grace subdues the pain
now smoldering;
I am unshackled.

Loved by Another
whispering to me,
"You will not be overcome."
He has set me free.

AFTERMATH

have to be honest. These days as the pain persists—disappearing and showing up again—I'm feeling a little defeated. I don't know what's true for me.
Chronic pain or whatever comes in between. Oh, to be sure, I'm seeking God
about this. But I wonder if he's tired of all my questioning and has turned the
volume down . . . or off. In reality, I'm tired of me, and I'm at the end of my rope.
Before I let go, I will go back once more to that wretched boat tossing in the storm
(Mark 6:45–51, John 6:16–21).

I wonder if the disciples had a plan when they got in the boat and put it
out to sea. They had to be exhausted, confused, and unnerved after the long
day they'd had with Jesus and all those hungry people. Maybe they went fishing
because they had missed a whole day of catch, or they just wanted to enjoy an
evening in their boat. Perhaps they looked forward to a hot meal and time to
think over the strange events of the day. Whatever their motive, they chose to
resume life as they knew it.

When we experience relief from our suffering, no matter what it's been—
grief, loneliness, sickness, pain, depression, or a dark period of doubt—our
normal course of action is to take action. Get back to life again! We are grateful
for the reprieve and wiser for it. To be lifted from the pit is miraculous, and we
want to live fully again.

This is where I have been stuck. What do I do after the pain?

> And after He had taken leave of them,
> He went up on the mountain to pray. (Mark 6:42)

Jesus had to be weary to the bone and spiritually drained after a day of pouring His Father's wisdom and compassion on all of those people. Now it was dusk, and everyone was gone, even the guys were off in their boat. He could rest and talk with His Father.

Still holding the rope above what looks like a really dark pit, I consider Jesus' plan. He spent time with His Father. Meanwhile, the storm was picking up out at sea. I believe Jesus knew that, and it was part of His conversation with God. As the Son rested with His Father, He was being given new instructions. "Walk on the sea."

I'm beginning to see a process of victory through suffering.

In the crucible of pain, what is the sufferer to do? Only one thing: surrender. I know for myself, I can do nothing in it, not even pray. This is when we give it all to God.

> My Father, if it is possible, may this cup be taken from me.
> (Matthew 26:39)

Jesus has been there with us.

What, then, do we do *with* our pain? Surely great sorrow, deep depression, and chronic pain will affect the way we live. This is where the real battle lies. Will our afflictions be the devil's gain, or do we remain in God's will? When we consider our Creator and all He has given us through the ages, praise pours through our weary spirit, glorious healing praise. This is what to do with pain—turn it into praise!

When the reprieve comes and pain subsides, there is a lift in the spirit, sunshine in the clouds, and the promise of a new day. Hope returns. How many times have I asked the LORD, "What now do I do *after* the pain?" I want to know what He wants me to do, and I wonder how I, so unreliable in my brokenness, could ever be of service.

"Abide."

This is what to do after all that pain, "Abide in Me and I with you" (John 15:4). Before He calmed the storm and took the boat to land, Jesus went to be alone with His Father.

As the branch cannot bear fruit by itself unless it abides in the vine,
so neither can you unless you abide in Me. (John 15:4)

There is a victory and purpose in suffering with God. Sometimes, it takes such a long time to understand and accept it, and often, we ride a wicked storm in what seems to be a boat with many leaks. There is always hope we cannot see, for surely it is Jesus with us in the tossing waves. He will bring us to shore where we can rest in Him. It is what we've learned in, with, and after our suffering that He knows and uses to glorify His Father. After we rest with Him, He will crown us with the fruit of our pain.

Purge me with hyssop, and I shall be clean, wash me
and I shall be whiter than snow. Let me hear joy of gladness;
let the bones You have broken rejoice. (Psalm 51:7–8)

SECTION IV
SEASONAL SNIPPETS

THIS IS YOUR NEW

As I write this, snow, like parade confetti, is swirling outside my window. It is a silent dusting of peace and nostalgia—a perfect end to the Christmas holidays, New Years, and Epiphany. Snippets of my childhood linger, reminding me of snow days, smothering coats, boots, and mittens, hot chocolate, and days out of school. Snow days after Christmas were a kid's dream come true!

Much later, when my children's eyes danced at the sight of falling snow on a school day and fought to get to their snowsuits and sleds, the weather was not at all fun for me. It was a sabotage of my tranquility and sanity. The holidays had left me in a pile of clutter, to-do lists, and at least five pounds of fat on my hips. It was time for those kids to get back to school and for me to get a fresh start again.

I wonder if Mary was frustrated when the three wise men showed up at her door, with their studded crowns, dirty sandals, and smelly clothes, not to mention those nasty camels doing what camels do in the yard? Here she was with her husband and a toddler, trying to keep house and protect her very special child from germs, falls, and neighborhood bullies. She needed to keep a quiet, clean home where God could bless her little one unhindered. Then there was a knock at the door, and guess who had come for dinner: three worldly strangers.

Of course, Mary didn't lose her cool or recommend a guesthouse down the street to the eager sages tripping over themselves, the donkeys, chickens, and lambs to get to her baby. Mary was in the presence of God, with His Spirit indwelling her, and full of the grace He had poured into her. Mary's life was new.

Every painting we have ever seen of this mother, her child, and the three visitors shows hospitality and motherhood at its best. Even after the wise men bade their farewells, leaving behind their treasures and mess, the mother of Jesus kept her peace. She did not slam the door behind them and run for the broom. She was with Jesus and that was enough.

What if an unexpected sandstorm blew in and the wise men had to remain in the small house with the family? What about the camels, the food, and the laundry? It would have been messy but worked out fine. They all were with Jesus, and it was a beautiful thing. You can just imagine the stories, prayers, and music.

Do you feel like you are out of grace and need a rest from kids, company, and Christmas? Are holiday memories clouding your vision? Are your New Year's resolutions scattered under the mess of it all?

Behold, I will do a new thing! (Isaiah 43:19)

What could Isaiah be writing to us about?

The week after Epiphany, should be a time of quiet reflection and gratitude. We, too, have been with Jesus. But our peace has been sabotaged by what we see, what we don't see, and what we're afraid to know. What are in front of us are piles of laundry, pine needles, scraps of wrapping paper, and ten unwanted pounds. Turning around, we find bills, emails, back-to-back appointments, and Christmas cards still to be mailed. Even a glistening snowfall won't divert the whirlwind before us.

Where do we go from here?

A better question is, "Where have we been?" Like the wise men, we have been with Jesus when we celebrated His birth on Christmas. He is with us—Immanuel—and He promises He will make all things new.

What is in front of us, the checkbook, dirty clothes, and Fitbit, may look the same, but it is all new creation in a brand new season. Just as Mary and Joseph cared for their baby and cleaned up after visitors, and the wise men saddled up their camels and trudged a different way home, we, too, are going about our drudgery and tasks. But we are made new!

This is the Good News! Yes, it is all new because we have God and He is the Creator of all things, making them new over and over, especially you and me.

Therefore if anyone is in Christ, the new creation has come!
The old is gone, the new is here! (2 Corinthians 5:17)

What you see in front of you is a fresh creation. And it is His. You don't have to make it look new. He has done it, and He is making you newer than ever before. "Arise, shine!" This is your new year—your new season—your new forever! You are beloved, beautiful, and bountiful in hope, joy, and love. You have no idea how beautiful you are, even in what appears to be chaos around you.

Look at it all and smile. Know that God has already made it new, and He promises His newness is not just for now, but:

I will make you majestic forever, a joy from age to age. (Isaiah 60:15b)

Yes, you are majestic today, a week from today, all year, and forever because you have been with Jesus and He has made you magnificently new!

MARY'S LOVE

Until this Easter season, I didn't know much about Mary of Bethany other than her sitting at the feet of Jesus, weeping when her brother died, and washing Jesus' feet with expensive oil at a dinner party. I knew that her inability to keep on task irritated her older sister and that Jesus had commended her for using precious oil for His feet.

Vicariously, I became infatuated and inspired by this loner who found company with Jesus and called Him Lord through my daughter who played Mary of Bethany's character in the Easter play, "The Man Called Jesus." During the eight weeks of intense practicing for the play, managing her home, corralling and homeschooling their five children, my daughter became a radiant lap-puppy for Jesus! What was it about Mary's character that gave my daughter transforming grace and joy?

Jesus owned Mary and Mary adored Jesus.

But one thing is needed, and Mary has chosen that good part,
which will not be taken from her. (Luke 10:42)

Once Mary found Jesus, her Teacher, she put herself in the front of the line and stayed there, riveted. She never said a word, just followed, watched, and listened. When He and the disciples joined her sister and brother for dinner, she was mesmerized to the point of being inhospitable. Whatever she heard from Jesus' lips sunk deep into her soul, changing her curiosity to revelation. Gentle, silent Mary became a passionate spiritual scholar as she sat at her Master's feet, learning of His will and His word. Never mind the chores, politics, state-of-affairs, or hierarchy: The Kingdom of God had come! Mary got it.

Mary never pressured Jesus, argued with Him, or questioned His plan. When her beloved brother died, and her sister railed and wailed at Jesus, Mary waited for Him. She fell at His feet when He arrived and wept of her trust in Him. Seeing her broken heart and the weeping of all those around her, Jesus wept and groaned for His people. Only Mary could have heard—and understood—her Lord's agony.

Mary and Jesus shared a bond that went beyond this world. The childlike woman who had been so reserved became confident, even bold in her faith. Mary spent so much time with the Man telling the truth about the Kingdom of God that she perceived the news of His impending death before any of His closest disciples. Six days before Jesus would be crucified, Mary demonstrated her trust in His purpose. She opened a jar of precious oil, which, in her familiar manner, she poured onto Jesus' feet then rubbed in with her hair. Despite objection from others around the table, Mary anointed her Lord, thus acknowledging what had been revealed to her (John 12:1–8). Mark records in his Gospel that Mary anointed Jesus' head with oil, an act that brought the highest commendation from Jesus:

> **What this woman has done will also be told as a memorial to her.**
> **(Mark 14:9)**

Mary gave Jesus all of herself and worshipped Him with all that she had. This may be the pure devotion Charles Wesley had in mind when he wrote,
"Oh, that I could forever sit,
Like Mary, at the Master's feet:
Be this my happy choice:
My only care, delight and bliss,
My joy, my Heaven on earth be this, to hear the Bridegroom's voice."

To know Mary of Bethany is to know how to love Jesus. Sit with Jesus as she did, drink His words, feel His Love, love Him back, and trust Him with every detail of your life.

Draw near to God and He will draw near to you. (James 4:7)

CALLED, LOVED, AND KEPT

When we attend graduation ceremonies, we go to applaud another's achievement. We marvel at the graduates' successes, such as that of our grandson, who received high awards in both academics and community service.

We, the attendees, have no idea the personal challenges, choices, or commitments the one celebrated made along the way (except for perhaps the parents, who made their own sacrifices on another level, usually behind closed doors). We see only bright smiling faces, and through our tears, we say, "Oh, I knew you would."

Yes, we felt certain our grandson, Gabriel Thomas, would receive high honors at his new high school, which he had only attended for his senior year. Gabe is a focused, persistent young man. Some say he is stubborn. When Gabe has a conviction, which he does about following Jesus Christ; a goal, which he did with academics; and purpose, as he has about serving God, like a bull in an arena with a red flag waving, he puts his head down and charges. He is an enigma of a kid—playful, wise, and steadfast, gentle in demeanor and fierce in spirit.

Does God call only those, like our Gabe and his Class of 2016 to pay attention to the future?

To our grandson and his graduating class, a speech was given that reached the celebratory audience, waking us from drifting memories and happy tears, to the life we are to live in Jesus Christ.

This was a message to take to heart.

The graduates and audience were given three words as anchors in a stormy world. They came from the Book of Jude, where the writer first proclaimed he was a servant.

This was not the first word we were told to remember, but it was foundational for the next three. A servant is what Christ was to all of mankind and what He called us to be. Before we can do anything worthwhile in this world, we must first be servants. Being a servant to Jesus Christ can be a monumental task for anyone, but especially to young adults about to be set free in the world. Serving and freedom do not mix. To those committed to Jesus Christ and His commission to "go out and make disciples of all nations . . . teaching them all I have commanded you," serving Him is not daunting; it is deliberate. Serving others is a mindset of humility and sacrifice.

Jude addressed the servants of Jesus Christ as being "called," the first word given to the graduates by their speaker. To be called is to be singled out, to stand alone, and to be accountable solely for oneself. This points to a powerful and ominous selection, particularly to a high school student who's grown up belonging to groups, teams, clubs, and ultimately, unified in one large graduating class. Suddenly, he or she is being called not to follow the group, look like everyone else, or hang with certain cliques but to stand alone.

Servants of Jesus Christ, young and old, are to realize the reality of our callings. Though we are in this world, we are not of it. We are separated for a cause: to share the Gospel by living it in our daily lives. "That," reminded our speaker, "means we are different."

Teenagers hearing these fearsome words would swallow hard, thinking about their place in a world that demands and advertises conformity. For the Christian, this is armor for battles ahead. Serving Christ means being strong in one's convictions, immovable in faith, and courageous in spirit. This calling also means we must be bold from the beginning, passionately announcing who we are in Jesus Christ.

The graduates were given sound practical advice.

"When you wake up every morning," the speaker directed, "ask yourself the Kingdom question. What is God's call on my life today?"

This is good counsel for us all. We are a distinguished people, chosen and called to serve in the Kingdom of God. We did not choose God. He chose us; our calling is not a choice but a command:

> Go and bear fruit and that your fruit should abide so that whatever you ask the Father in my name, He may give it to you. (John 15:16)

What can we do to make a difference in the world for Jesus Christ?

In his greeting, Jude refers to his readers as "beloved," for indeed God Himself loves us. The One who claims each of us as His own is Almighty God, Creator of all life, Alpha and Omega—the beginning and the end—our Father in Heaven who "formed my inward parts; knitted me together in my mother's womb . . . saw my unformed substance; in Your book were written . . . the days that were formed for me" (Psalm 139: 13,16).

What could give a young adult who knows Jesus and praying about future decisions more confidence than being told he is loved as David was? What other credentials would be more important to a job seeker? In college, the marketplace, or mission field, to be loved by God is all the validation one needs for success in the Kingdom.

Lest there be any doubt along life's journey when the ways and wiles of the world pull and tear at our hopes, dreams, and prayers, Jude reminds us that we are "kept" for Jesus Christ. It is Jesus who fights for us and sees that "all things work together for the good." (Romans 8:28) It is by God's power that His beloved is kept in the fold, never to be abandoned, and always cherished. With steadfast conviction, the Believer knows:

> Some trust in chariots, some trust in horses,
> but we trust in the name of the Lord our God. (Psalm 20:7)

"It pleases God to be your God," the graduates' speaker assured them. He then solemnly scanned the audience and asked, "Will you be His people?"

As Christians we are chosen, loved, and kept to glorify God in His Kingdom on earth and in heaven. Whether we are eighteen or eighty, this is to be our daily mission.

"Will you be His people today?"

Now to Him who is able to keep you from stumbling and to present you blameless before the presence of His glory with great joy, to the only God our Savior, through Jesus Christ our Lord, be glory, majesty, dominion, and authority before all time and now and forever. Amen. (Jude 24)

THE BRIDEGROOM'S TEARS

This summer, I attended a wedding that was a banquet of miracles. I, like most of the guests, was caught up with the emotion of the celebration, not only because the groom was my grandson, but also because his bride was breathtakingly beautiful. The sanctuary overflowed with friends and family who had come from all over to share the happy occasion. The nine bridesmaids were dressed in delicate, flowing gowns of blush, matching their glistening cheeks. The twelve groomsmen, boys tumbling and joking just the day before, were now men, hair combed and faces washed. They stood straight and tall in suits with crisp shirts, guarding the hopes and dreams of their best friend, the groom. The newlyweds, soaked in their love for one another, held hands at the altar as they bowed their heads and shared the Sacrament of Holy Matrimony. Who wouldn't get carried away with a wedding so enormously beautiful to the soul's senses?

Billy Graham once said, "The Bible stresses a marriage ideally should be a picture of a reflection of Christ's love for His people."

The gates of Heaven were thrown wide open in the sanctuary where Alec and Hannah were married. There, Christ welcomed us, His Bride—the Church—into His throne room as we gazed teary-eyed upon a couple who had given their lives first to God, promising to worship, obey and serve Him, and then to each other with the same love that Jesus pours forever upon His Church. Their honor to God and their devotion to one another brought such joy to our Father in Heaven that

He utterly gave us a reflection of His Holy Love. It was a miraculous intervention! Did we sense His presence?

How much, we ask, does Jesus love us, His bride? How beautiful, white, and pure are we as He gazes at us from His throne, surrounded by angels singing songs of abounding love, the melodies of which swirl in our hearts, inviting us to, "Come! See how much I adore you!"

If we turn away, pull back, or drop our heads, how it must break the heart of our Savior. Yet, He waits patiently for us to lift our eyes and smile radiantly as we say, "Yes! My groom, I am coming to You!"

Can you imagine the heart of Jesus exploding with love-filled joy and how He will receive us? This was the miracle we saw at the wedding that Saturday evening. Not one of us missed it.

When his bride appeared in the sanctuary, holding her father's arm and beaming radiantly in luminous white, the groom wept. All that he had ever wanted, prayed for, and hoped would come to pass was before him: His beloved! Wiping his tears and with joy unspeakable, he reached out to take the hand of his bride.

This is how Jesus reaches for us, with the tears of a groom for His bride with love that will never let us go. We are His Church, His Bride. The groom may have wept, but the tears were those of God's for His Beloved.

Blessed are those who are invited to the marriage supper . . .
These are the true words of God. (Revelation 19:9)

FOREVERMORE

Fifty-four years is a long time to live with one person. For my husband and me, these years have included career changes, financial adjustments, illnesses, celebrations, and the ongoing miraculous expansion of our family. Together, we have experienced joy, anger, confusion, and abject awe of the One who orchestrated it all. Through it, we have stayed together because God Almighty has bound us with His love. We have seen His miracles and mercies for almost five decades, and we are still learning about the commitment of marriage.

Dan and I were married five months after we met, during which time he went on three short cruises, and I moved to another town with my family. We were married in December 1966 because Dan was scheduled to deploy in January.

If you think five months of sporadic dating is not long enough to know someone well enough to get married, you are right. But God answers the prayers of those who call on Him—sometimes even before.

Our first fight came a week after our wedding day when I wanted to drive, and Dan wouldn't let me. The good news was, rather than going to sea on a carrier for a month, as we had expected, we were driving to Pensacola, Florida, where he would begin Flight Training. As newlyweds, we would be able to set up our first home together. Funny how that worked out. I had not yet known to ask God for this, but He was already in our marriage.

While Dan trained to become a fighter pilot over the following years, I learned how to keep house, become a mother, and be a Navy wife. This combination of Top Gun versus babies versus drama queen was spiraling toward disaster, so I threw temper-tantrum-laced prayers at God. He chose to intervene by being closer than just the recipient of my fits; He showed up in the Person of Jesus Christ.

I will be brutally frank; Jesus Christ saved our marriage. It had nothing to do with my weeping and wailing, our adorable daughters, Dan's one thousand carrier landings, or how madly (pun intended) in love we were. Jesus Christ taught us how to love one another as He does His Church.

After I accepted Him (begged Him, to be exact) as my Personal Savior, Jesus threw at me (He had to be tough and fast) 1 Peter 3 in my brand-new King James Bible, which now is as wrinkled and withered as I am.

> Likewise, ye wives, be in subjection to your own husbands;
> that if any obey not the word, they also may without the word be won
> by the conversation of the wives; while they behold your chaste
> conversation coupled with fear. (1 Peter 3:1–2 KJV)

Translated: "Beloved, stop whining. Smile. Leave the rest to Me."

Because I wanted Dan to have the freedom and joy I felt in my new faith, I was happy to comply with any suggestion Jesus offered. With uncommon calm and contentment, I made my husband's breakfasts before pre-dawn flights and dinners after his late-night Happy Hours. I tried to hold back my tongue and tears and made an effort to keep the house neat. By then, we had two little girls, and I was pregnant again. Dan was gearing up for his fourth deployment in seven years. My lady's Bible study kept me balanced. Jesus is a smart and timely Savior.

Meanwhile, Dan did not object to the Bible I left in full view on the table. He joined our elementary-style table graces and attended church with our kids and me whenever he was home. These were not easy adjustments for a fighter pilot who didn't know Jesus. But God heard my fervent prayers and, knowing my husband's deepest needs, He brought Dan into our fold, and we became one in the family of Christ.

Fast-forward five decades. One would think by now I would have learned the secrets of a good marriage and could perhaps teach on the matter. But recently,

I attended a Bible study with younger women, including my daughter, and was deservedly convicted when the group's leader, practically a child, shared her own humbling advice about marriage. She had been under a lot of pressure keeping up with the needs and demands of her children, meeting the schedule of the Bible study curriculum, and preparing to give her testimony to its leadership when her husband basically shut down, probably from his own work stress. Tears streaming down her cheeks, this beautiful young woman of God shared, "I have always prayed for our home to be a safe haven for our family, where we can lay down our burdens and rest without fear of condemnation." She then thanked God for her husband who worked hard for his family and trusted them enough to find release at home. What grace God had given to this Christ-filled wife!

I wish I could tell you this was something I had known. It is not. But because of the humility and submissive spirit of a woman nearly half my age, I have been inspired to also make my home a "safe haven." It is never too late to learn.

Dan and I are now approaching the "forevermore" of our marriage vows and we are discovering we need new guidelines, ones that will lead us into eternity. Like the house we have lived in for almost twenty years, a few of our structural units have had to be replaced, a little remodeling and painting is needed to keep looks updated, and the parties we plan are spaced further apart on the calendar.

We are learning to live together in a new season.

I have arthritis and back issues: Dan has sore feet and a choosey stomach. I walk the dogs, fold the laundry, and still make great pasta dishes. Dan makes the bed, carries the laundry downstairs, and fills my flowerpots with soil. I make sure he doesn't eat mayonnaise or processed bread and boil dozens of eggs for him to eat instead of chips. When I am crippled with back spasms, he stops anything he is doing to help do what is necessary to ease the pain.

God has given us the grace to laugh at our embarrassing moments, enjoy our slower pace, make fun of the crookedness of all our forty fingers and toes, and hold each other when things just hurt. He has not abandoned us.

Dan and I thank God with words hard to express for the abundant blessings He has poured upon our family. Our testimony of His faithfulness is our marriage and our children and our grandchildren who "love the Lord with all of their heart and soul."

We have learned that at times, marriage is hard, but it is holy; it is work, but it is worthy; it is challenging, but it is cherished. It is a commitment God designed for the man and woman He chose since the beginning of time. He binds them together in His Love, that they may be one throughout eternity.

. . . that they may be one just as We are One. (John 17:22)

SUMMER LOVE

Summertime to me means grandkids. All of our grandchildren learned how to swim in our backyard pool, so it is a no-brainer that they return to it year after year.

They have an ongoing contest, in which the girls participate only half-heartedly, to see who can be the first one in the pool for the year. First, it was Alec then Gabe, Childers, and next year, Hunter will probably be the brave Polar Pool Jumper. After this traditional contest, our yard and house become a circus, cut loose with kids everywhere. This is the summertime I look forward to.

Pool days have their drawbacks, mind you. Sometimes, it is overwhelming and exhausting. So much hilarity and drama mixed up with sopping bathing suits, dripping popsicles, and sodden towels are both fabulous and frazzling. Meanwhile, the clock is ticking, the minutes passing, and those fantastic children are growing up. Gratitude and joy fill my heart when the kids, with their noise and mess, surround me as I try desperately to savor the moments. I don't want to miss the miracle of the children.

"Maybe their time with me will be some of their favorite memories!" I find myself hoping. When they are gone, I sit surveying the stillness before me and wonder how soon they will be back. Though I am a little weary these days after the children leave, they still invigorate me with memories of their joy-filled lives.

Reflecting on the coming and going of our grandchildren and how I scurry around trying to please each one with a PB&J here, a towel there, an orange popsicle for this one, and a purple popsicle for that one, never actually connecting with any of them, I think of how I find myself dashing around in my head trying and wanting to please God with whatever I think would make Him happy.

Will grandmothers ever learn?

It is far too easy to get over-stimulated when approaching God. A visit with God should be a peaceful and quiet time when we connect with Him. Often, the communing becomes conversing —a push-pull complaint. "You said," we pray, then add "I tried" or "I'm trying," and the prayer becomes a petition when we truly just wanted His presence.

Unfortunately, intervening thoughts can create a cacophony of requests, regrets, confessions, and professions while, in between, intrusions of alarm, anxiety, and angst are like children running amuck through the house with dripping towels. It is so hard to concentrate on the glory of God when an empty wallet, scrolling newsflashes, and sharks at the beach clamor about us. Like the sigh of my heart wanting to hold tightly to the moments with my grandchildren, I cry out to God to fill me with His Spirit when I pray. I don't want to miss His presence or forget His goodness.

Be still and know that I am God. (Psalm 46:10)

Yes, we try to be still within the noise. But we talk too much and try too hard. God tells us He speaks to those voices. "BE STILL!" our heavenly Father commands our efforts to please Him and those worries that we never will.

Almighty God raises His sword of truth and silences the lies that tell us He's not listening, we're dispensable, and all we've lived for will be forgotten. With His voice, confliction, conviction, and apprehension go out the way they came in. When God commands stillness, He does housekeeping in our heads.

We can still pray when we are riding a bike, mowing the lawn, or wiping ice cream from the kitchen floor. It is most wonderful to be communing with God while sitting on a mountaintop, gazing at a sunset, or in a stolen moment in the laundry room, but it is not necessary to have the perfect moment to be with God. God is perfect in *every* moment. Whenever we turn our hearts to God, we need only acknowledge Him as Who He is. When we do, we exalt Him—we praise Him —and immediately, we are within His presence.

He says, "I will be exalted among the nations,
I will be exalted in the earth!" (Psalm 46:10)

"It's like," as I told my oldest grandson (the first to have won the Polar Pool Jump) when he called me on his birthday, "when I am with you kids, I am frenzied by all I think I need to do for you. Likewise, when I try to be with God, I am distracted by everything I need to say and ask. It is after the house is quiet and the last of the pool raiders have shut the front door when I realize I have been surrounded by love—a love so boisterous and bountiful it fills me with joy and renewed vitality, even as I pick up the wet towels!"

My wise Alec agreed, "Yes, MomMom. There are days when we try to see God and can't seem to find Him, even in prayer. We just need to open our eyes wider and see how He has been there all along."

It is true: No matter what the season, I see God clearly in the love and goodness of my grandchildren. Though, admittedly, summer is the most fun!

For the Lord is good; His steadfast love lasts forever,
and His faithfulness to all generations. (Psalm 100:5)

SAVOR THE GRATITUDE AND PASS THE GRAVY

"Thanksgiving is just another day to us. We'll probably go out for shrimp. Yes, it's just another day."

I knew what my dejected friend was really saying since her children and grandchildren lived too far away to come home for Thanksgiving. What she meant was, "We just want to get past the day."

I pondered her statement, feeling that most of our family would be around our table on Thanksgiving Day. I was too excited about our home being filled with family in just a few days to be distracted by her remorse. I promised I would pray for her.

If my family was not coming for Thanksgiving, the dining room table stayed dusty and bare, and if no turkey was roasting in the oven, would I, too, brush off the holiday, trying to get rid of it? For unavoidable and unexpected reasons, many people find themselves alone on Thanksgiving. Just last week, a carrier battle group carrying some 7,500 men and women deployed to the Middle East for an extended period, leaving their families to celebrate Thanksgiving and several more holidays without them. Will they choose to eat shrimp instead of turkey or just try to ignore the day? Does the menu really matter as long as we are giving thanks?

The extraordinary thing about Thanksgiving Day is that it was founded on the idea of giving God gratitude for His provision and protection. It is a whole day to just be thankful! When we are surrounded by our loved ones, sitting at a table decorated with a cornucopia, and inhaling mouthwatering morsels of turkey, stuffing, and gravy, we give thanks for our family, home, and good food. But do we consider from Whom all this bounty and joy came? Whether in a crowded room with our loved ones or alone with our memories, do we thank Him enough?

If we were to truly grasp all that God has provided and how He has blessed us, it wouldn't matter if we ate turkey or shrimp on Thanksgiving Day; we would fall on our knees in worship.

Thanksgiving is active gratitude for all God does and all He is. It is praising Him for memories of provision and fulfillment, thanking Him for His presence and protection every day, and acknowledging Him for Who He is.

Years ago, we opened our home to a young man who had hit rock bottom and needed a family to help get him back on his feet. We gave him our daughter's room redecorated into a guy cave, included him in our family routine, and spent hours at the kitchen table talking with him about the love of Jesus.

That Thanksgiving when our new friend was with us, I wanted to do something different, so I could hear a chorus of "thank yous" from everyone around our food-laden table, rather than the typical "amen" after the blessing, followed by "pass the gravy!" I decided the best way to elicit such a joyful response was for me to find a special gift to give to each of our three daughters, my husband, and our guest. That was such fun for me, "The Present Lady."

On Thanksgiving Day, I placed a brightly wrapped gift on the table in front of each plate and called everyone to dinner. Confusion changed to delight on their faces as my family sat down in front of their presents.

I announced my reason for the unusual gift-giving. "This year, I decided to give each of you a gift on Thanksgiving because I am so grateful to God for each of you here at this table!"

As the presents were unwrapped, I heard the symphony I had been waiting for:

"Thank you!"

"Oh, wow! Thanks!"

"Thank you so much!" My heart filled up with their praises, and I felt an inkling of how God must feel when we so joyfully and enthusiastically give Him our gratitude for His blessings.

When I glanced over to our guest, who was unfolding the shirt I had carefully selected for him, he was looking down, sort of shaking his head.

"Do you like it?" I asked quietly.

His eyes scanned the table covered with holiday bounty, surrounded by the happy faces of a family who had given him acceptance and love over the past several months. Was he allowing himself to be happy once again?

Smiling, he quietly responded, "I guess I never expected this. I've never seen anything quite like it. I don't know how to thank you."

That humble gratitude hit me like thunder. The love of God—have we ever seen anything quite like it? In our wildest dreams, did we expect the magnificent glory, power, and greatness of God, who made the heavens and earth and sea and all that has ever been in them, to actually be present in our lives? Have we ever known anything at all that wraps around us like the extravagant love of God our Father? How could we even begin to thank Him enough?

Let us give gratitude worthy of Him this Thanksgiving, no matter where we are or with whom we share the day. Make our giving of thanks active! Let every "thank you," whether it is for the passing of gravy or a smile from a waitress, be a genuine expression of thanks to the One who is the Giver of all of our joys, both past and present, and whose Presence will be with us throughout eternity.

Whether you eat or drink, or whatever you do, do all to the glory of God.
(1 Corinthians 10:31)

GOD'S GIFT LIST

It doesn't seem fair that the Christmas season, so full of celebration and good-will, brings with it stress, short-tempers, and exhaustion. The holiday chaos has nothing to do with the meaning of Christmas. Despite the fact the essence of the Christmas celebration is "Christ is born!" and "God is with us!" we leave Him behind as we scurry about doing our shopping, gifting, and entertaining. No matter how hard we try to scale down the holiday schedule, new obligations and unexpected mishaps foil our best-laid plans. There have been too many years of my adult life when December 1st signaled a twenty-five-day marathon, with flickering Advent candles at the finish line.

A few years ago, I realized that part of my holiday havoc was my penchant for perfect gifting. I love giving presents and strive to think of and search for mean-ingful Christmas gifts. While gift-giving is a good thing, its symbolic purpose is more important. We give presents to others because God gave His greatest gift to us: His Son. So for Christmas, shouldn't we first give a gift to God?

How can we, mere humans with our heads just above the wrapping paper, give anything of worth to the King of kings? What can we give the One who gave to us eternal life?

In short, we can give God our presence.

When our Lord looks at us, He sees the gifts of the Spirit, which He has poured into us: love, joy, peace, hope, kindness, and humility. He does not see us pulling our hair out, racing through traffic, haggling over sale prices, or snapping at our kids. God sees within us His Son and hearts that truly want to serve Him.

In Your presence is fullness of joy (Psalm 16:11)

I have discovered that when I start each day of the holidays with God, they seem brighter, richer, and more purposeful. Because God unwraps the gifts He put in my spirit like compassion and mercy, opportunities to share these gifts seem to appear out of nowhere. No longer does the day's To-Do List control my schedule because I have the sense of a Holy agenda.

When the Christmas Season seems overwhelming and demanding to you, present yourself in prayer to God at the beginning of each day and ask Him how He wants you to use His gifts. Invite a struggling family to dinner? Visit someone feeling lonely? Help a single mom wrap Christmas presents? Take chili to the volunteer firemen? Bake cookies for community workers? Make a date with new friends to attend church and go to lunch? Send boxes of gifts to an orphanage? Commit to praying for those who struggle in spiritual darkness?

God's list of gifts goes on and on, wrapped in the true spirit of Christmas—sharing His Son, Immanuel, with the world.

WELCOME TO YOUR WORLD

O n Christmas Day too many years ago, a chunky baby boy with golden hair was born. Coffee cups were left behind on tables, wrapping paper and gift boxes were strewn around the family room, and the unlit Christmas tree looked slightly dehydrated. Our entire family—fathers, mothers, children, aunts, uncles, and cousins—were gathered at the hospital to welcome a Christmas baby into our world. With gusto and appetite, Hunter Charles left his only known home of amorphous tranquility to join a new sphere of lights, noises, surfaces, and the touching, turning, and cradling of hands holding him in the very air he gulped. The baby's wail brought forth a fresh onslaught of cacophony from the blurred shadows hovering around him. This bewildered newborn seemed to know he was at the mercy of a new world, and he wanted to go back home.

Hunter is now a robust, sensitive, and introspective child. His mop of red hair is as bright as his blue eyes are deep. He stops at no obstacle bigger, harder, or faster than himself, yet he tip-toes over sand, cringes at the feel of grass, and panics at the sight of a facecloth. While Hunter's older brother is quick with words, confident, and athletic, Hunter speaks from observation, prefers fun to competition, collects rocks, and nurtures his hamster, Rosie. Being with Hunter feels a little like opening a Christmas present.

When I think about the birth of Jesus, I can't help but wonder what it must have been like for Him to leave the ethereal glory of Heaven, where His company included the encompassing love of His Father and a legion of illuminated angels extolling praises as far as He could hear. What did the crash through the eternal hemisphere feel like as the needles of straw met Him on the manger? Unlike Hunter, Jesus did not come from the world. God gave Him to the world. Yet this baby was born in a manger among animals, shepherds, strangers, and eventually kings. He, too, gave his first lusty cry, learned to suckle, and felt the chill of night. From the moment of His birth, the Son of God was immersed in the world as the Son of Man.

Christmas Day brings double celebration in our household. The birthday cake for Jesus, decorated with candies and candles, is now shared with Hunter. "Happy Birthday Jesus and Hunter!" sung loud and clearly reflects in a boisterous way the joy and gratitude of our family. As we've watched Hunter grow from infant to boyhood, we are reminded that Jesus, too, crawled on floors, splashed in puddles, and prayed at bedtime.

God came to earth as an infant, holy and pure, and as we celebrate His birth we are reminded that He truly was with us, lived among us, and is now within us.

DO YOU WANT TO HOLD THE BABY?

No need to be quiet. You don't have to tiptoe. Just walk right in with your open heart. What you see has been waiting for you and is very much awake!

Ever so gently, pick up your Bible. Do you sense its weight pulsing in your hands? Pull back the cover and caress the pages. Listen to the story of God whispering through your fingers.

Can you imagine your Bible being the Christ Child in your hands?

How would it feel to put your arms around Baby Jesus and cradle Him? Would you tremble knowing He is the Messiah? Think of touching this infant ever so gently and sliding back the cloth draping His head. Imagine stroking the downy hair, smiling at the brows, like etchings of dove feathers sweeping above His eyes.

Do you think Mary would let you hold her new baby? Perhaps, as she lifted Him to you, she would whisper His name, "Jesus. Our baby's name is Jesus," her eyes filled with wonder.

Yes, He is *our* Baby.

This Baby in your arms would be warm, clinging as if it had always belonged there, next to your heart. If the sleeping Messiah woke, peering about the stable trying to focus, and He found you looking down at Him, His gaze so deep and knowing, it would pierce your heart. In His eyes, you would see love, as you've never known, and you would see that He has always known you. In fact, He has been waiting for you. With your heart beating next to His, the history of the world would lose its sorrow and you would sense the peace of eternity.

Our Baby Jesus visits us all year round because He has entered our hearts, and we may behold Him every day. The Christmas season is an especially nice time to embrace the Holy Child in your Bible.

The Bible is God with us, Immanuel. With the Book of Life in your hands, you are holding the breathing, everlasting Word of God. The Bible imparts His life to us. As we read of the Creation, the Flood, the Flight, Prophets, Psalms, the Promise, and the Birth, we can feel the beat of the heart of God. Like the infant wrapped in swaddling clothes, our Bibles—bound in paper, cardboard, synthetic leather, or cowhide—pulsate with God's majesty!

This Christmas season, give yourself the joy of cradling the Holy infant in your hands. During the days of holiday preparation and celebration, pick up your Bible as if it was the baby in the manger and let His life melt your heart. Embrace His story, revere His presence, and caress the pages of His life.

Yes, you may hold Baby Jesus anytime! He is yours.

In the beginning was the Word and the Word was with God,
and the Word was God. (John 1:1)

REVIVAL OF THE RECYCLED

would have preferred to think of myself as recycled art rather than a discarded road sign. Yet, there was nothing salvageable about my journey-worn frame the other day as my daughter pulled her van—bulging with pillows, tote bags, rolling cases, stuffed animals, boogie boards, and blankets—out of the driveway. Her children, my life's bounty, bound in steel-plated car seats by straps from shoulder to crotch and back again, locked together with iron jaw buckle teeth that snap those babies into place, warning: "Authorized release only." I am not authorized; believe me. My granddaughters were secure for the trip home, this menagerie of whirlwind and clutter, my entire beating heart wrapped in their curls and blue eyes. An arsenal of water bottles, sippy cups, Goldfish, cereal bars, and the beacon of security itself, a cell phone with charger, was placed within the ready reach of the driver—my daughter, Mom.

Who needs road signs these days?

Our three daughters are much better mothers than I ever thought to be, let alone knew how to be. I've learned this is a common phenomenon among my friends who are also somewhat intimidated by their daughter's maternal prowess. Heaven knows we worked hard enough in the days before daycare, pre-preschool, play dates, and Girl's Night Out. We taught our children nursery school rhymes, kept up with their shots, paid quarters for their baby teeth, drove them to activities, and chaperoned them when necessary. All of this before Pampers, Pak 'n Plays, and DVDs. We fed them as we were instructed: milk, pureed jar food, peanut butter and jelly, French fries, and coke. Green beans and carrots were mixed in somewhere. Amazingly, the kids grew straight with arms, legs, fingers, and toes in place.

Our role models, our mothers, offered us aprons, mashed potatoes, and Dr. Spock, none of which worked well in our two-car, microwave-dinner and *Sesame Street*-equipped households. We had to be creative, think quickly, and pray for the best. I once even tethered our own two-year-old daughter to a tree in the front yard so she could play outside while I took care of the baby inside. When Daddy was at sea, we ate cereal for dinner and slept snuggled in my bed together. My suitcase stuffed with diapers, I took our one-year-old to Europe to follow my Navy husband's ship from port to port, leaving her with newly acquainted babysitters when necessary. I have even been known to leave a child or two in the car when I dashed into the grocery store. *Please God, forgive me.*

No wonder my daughters won't let me load their dishwashers. I cannot be trusted. Plus, I have no sanitizer in my purse. Grudgingly, I have acquiesced to washing my hands long enough to sing the main lines from "Happy Birthday," and I encourage and wait for each of the grandchildren to do the same while I hum.

In my bathroom, I supply hand towels, paper towels, guest towels, wipes, hand sanitizer, bar soap, liquid soap, and three types of hand lotion. The condition of the hands, a fertile ground for germs of the worst kind, I've been warned repeatedly, is a high priority, and I work hard to show my daughters my weapons. Yet, I have been known to leave a smear of peanut butter on a knife I've placed in the dishwasher, proving my lack of attention to cleanliness. That they allow me to clean the kitchen so often after the PB&Js, juices, Goldfish, cheese straws, pretzels, chips, macaroni and cheese, smoothies, and cinnamon oatmeal is truly a tribute of their tolerance for a worn-out "STOP" sign like me.

I used to be the one with all the answers, directions, corrections, and even predictions. I probably knew as much as Google. The kids obeyed, listened, and learned because I was the Mom, and I told them so. Our daughters are grown up now and don't need my directives or directions anymore. They have Google, Facebook, Instagram, and blogs. Often, I have to ask *them* for advice. Really, there's nothing in my stash of warnings that tells me when and when not to let a kid ride in the car without a car seat or when and how much sunscreen to apply . . . not even how to hook up a baby monitor. My "No!" is lost somewhere in the bag with "Stop!" so I default to "Yes, of course, you can!" to the children.

When I said, "Stop!" to my kids, I meant it, and they knew it. Stop playing with your food, stop teasing your sister, stop arguing. When the behavior warranted ceasing, my "Stop!" was heeded. "STOP!" followed by the perpetrator's full name, middle included, in my slightly frantic, elevated voice instantly signaled danger, halted all activity, and kept my children safe.

I was challenged at first when the babies became persons with opinions who questioned my authority. So, I threw in "Caution," "Advisory," and even "Yield" signals to help them with their choices and decisions. Sometimes "Stop" didn't allow them to travel their paths. They'd get lost occasionally, as we all do. Like a billboard beside the highway, I'd say, "Stop feeling remorse, guilt, and regret about things you can't change." "Merge and Proceed with Caution" was my advice as I guided our three little girls into adulthood.

Now I want to tell them, "STOP!" already with the cell phone, iPad, and all devices that suck in eyes, ears, and brain cells, "Look! Listen! Pedestrian Crossing!" Always glued to the activities, advice, and discoveries of their friends and their friends' friends being transmitted on their smartphones, my daughters miss the traffic circling them. With highly developed multi-task skills, they interact with their children's activities while carrying on long conversations on their handheld devices. The children are used to seeing their mother's heads bent down to the card-sized box and seem fine with it. That's what's important. Besides, that smart little box also holds games galore for the kids to enjoy when Mommy is talking in real life.

After my daughter pulled her van out of the driveway, I sat out on my deck strewn with bunched-up towels and pool toys. I heard occasional chirping from birds high up in the trees as I read about an amazing project created by art students from Allegheny College. Since I was feeling like a faded sign, lying beside a long stretch of highway that read, "Don't Stop. Move On," my spirits picked up.

Signs and Flowers is a garden of twelve large flowers made from discarded road signs and landscaping in the PennDOT storage lot in Meadville, Pennsylvania. In the spring and summer of 2001, the art students from Allegheny College designed and constructed the "garden," which has now become a popular tourist attraction while beautifying one of their busiest intersections. Out of recycled road signs, the students had designed a gateway of whimsical welcome to a town! The stamp-sized pictures I clicked on, one by one, mushroomed into kaleidoscopic gardens of merry flowers.

Suddenly, I realized if trashed signs can be made into tulips and daisies, I, too, could be recycled. What was it that God wanted me to do with the materials still intact in my life, and how could I rewire and reattach the fading roles I've played? Like those recycled signs, could I be revived?

In the Book of Isaiah, I read, "I dwell in the high and holy place, and also with him who is of contrite and lowly spirit to revive the heart of the contrite." (Isaiah 57:19)

The truth hit me like a truck. I didn't need to be recycled. Truth be known: That had already happened. Isn't that what grandmothers are? Recycled moms? What I needed was a revival, a complete, refreshing, restoring, and renewing of my spirit. That was exactly what God said He would do for me: "Revive my heart." I didn't need to settle for recycling. New wine does not do well in old wineskins.

But new wine is put into fresh wineskins, and so both are preserved.
(Matthew 9:17)

I may not be able to unbuckle a car seat, say no to a child, resist serving ice cream for breakfast or keep up with miniature Mario games, but I can read Bible stories, take care of the grandfather, spoil my dogs, and create fairy gardens. I can give my grandchildren a new vocabulary with words like "miragical" (a portmanteau for magical and miracle), and I can carry my cell phone so when my daughters call for advice, I'll be there. Rather than propping signs at my front door, I can hang waving flags displaying drawings from every season with "WELCOME HOME" painted in neon colors. Most important of all, I can storm the heavens with prayers for each one of my precious grandchildren and I can leave them with a legacy of faith.

Discarded no more, I will be discovered: a grandmother in new wineskin!

CELEBRATED WORSHIP

Celebrations are my family's signature activity. We memorialize, signify, and edify any event, accomplishment, or even slightly new behavior with gatherings, meals, noisemakers, and gifts. We try to never miss an opportunity to celebrate life.

For a family that has grown to eighteen members over fifty-four years, this party fetish has produced some pretty outlandish and unforgettable festivities. They have taken place at a huge variety of venues: rodeos, sports centers, ice cream parlors, the beach, the pool, and even on a small island of sand. Sometimes, our gatherings are intimate with just the grown-ups around the table; more often, the grandkids are included, which pushes the noise level over the top. The times we open the doors to extended relatives and friends, our celebrations take on the galaxy.

This year, we wanted to take our family celebration to a new level. We were facing some big transitions with my husband's retirement just months ahead, one family moving farther away, teenagers becoming college students, and for the first time, all members of the entire family were out of Pull-ups. This, in itself, called for a holiday!

We decided our "graduation" present should be a two-week vacation on the beach at the Outer Banks. It would be there that we could converge and celebrate the memories of all of the blessings God had bestowed upon us over the long haul. We had made it this far, through desert and glacier, without war or famine. It would be in a beach house made for almost two dozen, where we could honor one another—brothers, sisters, cousins, parents, and grandparents, in the best way of all—by spending time with each other without the disrupting distractions of the world. The seashore would unite our hearts and souls.

Waking up to golden sunrises melting across the ocean like candles on a cake made each day a gift. It seemed God Himself was excited about the joy we would find in it. With nothing else on our agenda other than to eat, swim, play, visit, and eat again, we absorbed ourselves in our collective interests and idiosyncrasies. Dressed in flip-flops, bathing suits, shorts, and tees, we were finely dressed for the culmination of years lived. Sitting around the huge dinner table was a rollicking group of folks of all ages with one common bond—family and the One who had covered it. With (very) loud voices, singing, laughing (we even danced), we celebrated each other and the reason why we were together. God had ordained it.

It was in the mornings, shortly after those glistening sun-streams, that I learned a new thing about worship. Having slept soundly in the aftermath of laughter, bantering, Scrabble, and *Star Wars*, I fairly leaped to the beach as the sun crept over the cresting waves. To match the generous beauty of the heaving ocean and foam-filled waves before me with eloquent gratitude was the motivation behind my early strolls. And, in the din of the sea's breath, I hoped my worship with God along the beach would keep our celebration perfect, not only for the time we were together but for the future.

I heard nothing from the Almighty, only the ocean rolling from depths to the shores I strolled. I walked and thought, prayed and wondered, hummed, and listened. Nothing. Looking out beyond the rising horizon, up at the forever blue sky, noting hovering pelicans skimming in unison over playful waves, I finally entertained my eyes on the interminable line of houses on the other side of the beach. How easily my conscience got pulled to the three-four- even five-storied houses painted in rainbow colors and perched proudly upon numbered sand dunes, their luminous windows as tall as buildings reflecting the glazed sky. It was hard not to let my thoughts wander to the celebrations being held in those glass castles.

The only sound from God I heard was, "Uh, hello?" which, obviously was not His voice but did show some smarts on my part. I had risen early to be with my Lord, and there I was drooling over manmade sea castles.

Turning my eyes back to the ocean, I literally halted in my tracks from the shock that hit my soul. *Oh!* The indescribable grandeur before me! The sky was a silken canopy hemmed with a silver thread as the ocean fathoms pushed satiny strokes of gilded blue toward me until, mesmerized, I felt the shock of swirling ruffled water playing at my ankles. It was like seeing eternity, itself, and almost touching it.

Suddenly, I realized the privilege before me—worship. The mere solitary act of tearing away from the present to opening all desires to God was to be immersed in Him in such a way there were no words, only breath and wonder. *Here* is where God is worshipped.

Celebrations have as many phrases, songs, and costumes as their countless celebrities, events, and traditions demand. Celebration is what God has gifted to us to give sound and action to our worship. It is what reminds us of our past, what we do in the present, and decorates hope for the future. Celebration is the catalyst to speechless, prostrating, numbing worship to the One who brought it all to pass. Only in worship, as our souls fill with God's glory, do we know His smile and have an inkling of His everlasting love.

When we celebrate, we find worship; when we worship, we find God.

By the end of our vacation and fourteen days of celebrating, we were a sun-crusted and somewhat frazzled family. Perhaps there is such a thing as too much celebrating! With sand stuck in unmentionable crevices, hair matted down, and coolers bulging with leftovers, we hugged our fond goodbyes, even though we were all returning to our neighborhoods close by. I knew, sadly enough, that once back in the real world, life would do its pulling, and seasons would claim their transitions.

Suddenly, our soon-to-be ten-year-old grandson grabbed me, eyes shining, "MomMom! Let's all have a family birthday party at your house. NEXT WEEK!"

Thus, it was planned, and we celebrated once again. God loves His parties and how we love to celebrate in unison with Him! And, when we worship, we worship Him in Spirit, where the agenda and venue are His alone.

Celebrate God all day, every day. I mean revel in Him! (Philippians 4:4, MSG)

WELCOME TO YOUR MISSION FIELD

A couple of weeks ago, on one of those Saturday afternoons when the world looked as if God had been on a cleaning spree the whole rainy week before, my husband and I attended a wedding in Richmond at a grand church, one sprawled over lush slopes and tucked in by elegant homes and manicured lawns. The opulence of the church and neighborhood suggested their budget did not often come up short, and among many other things, support for worldwide missions was probable. However, the message on the church's simple and tastefully placed exit sign, which we noticed when we departed the wedding ceremony, heralded that the heart of Christ's Great Commission was throbbing within.

WELCOME TO YOUR MISSION FIELD

What struck me was the focus of the missions—the field outside its doors. What a perfect place to hone servant skills: in the neighborhood, businesses, homes, and even during social events within the community.

These are the places where doing missionary work can become messy, testy, and toilsome.

The missionary's secret is truly being able to say, "I am His, and He is accomplishing His work and His purposes through me." It doesn't matter where or how

God engineers our circumstances; what matters is that we accept everything as His directive to bring Him into every situation. If we can't do the task before us in the kitchen, office, coffee shop, or bank, then, we aren't ready to sacrifice lifestyle, family, or finances in mission fields abroad.

Karl and Julie, an extraordinary couple with missionary hearts, were missionaries in Cape Town, South Africa years ago, where they set up housekeeping just outside Ocean View, a desperate community of shanties. With their three little girls in tow, they carried Christ's commission to "be witnesses of Me" by going into the poverty-stricken, drug-wrecked village to pull out sick babies, lost children, beleaguered women, and wasted men and bring them to Jesus.

Karl, an avid soccer player, organized soccer training camps and leagues to lure the boys from their troubles to learn a new game, team play, and leadership, along with stories of a man called Jesus who would be their champion forever.

Managing a home equipped with snakes, tarantulas, and rats—rather than a microwave, food processor, or icemaker—and raising her children (one with Downs Syndrome,), Julie grappled daily with the question of how to raise a family reflecting God's standard and provision. She used the weapons God provided for her in this rough-hewn home—instruction, fellowship, encouragement, and prayer. As God met her needs, she, in turn, brought His solutions, practiced through trial and error, to the community of women surrounding her. These women had no families, husbands, or child support to help them with their sick, malnourished, and wailing babies. Groups of girls and mothers became friends as they rocked their babies, shared childcare, learned how to make formula, practiced sanitation, and sang lullabies, such as "Jesus Loves Me This I Know."

After Julie gave birth to her third child, God impressed upon her the need for the village's single mothers to have a way to earn money to keep their babies healthy and safe in a society offering scant amounts of medicine and vaccines and harboring child traffickers. Julie's God-given talent is creativity, which she turned into a business. In a cheery, promised-filled room furnished with tables and rented sewing machines, women of Ocean View sew celebratory buntings with colorful fabrics sent from Julie's friends and family in the United States.

While Karl, Julie, and their girls brought Christ to Cape Town, their mission was clear, but then the family was called to a new mission field: home.

Karl's mother's cancer had returned with a vengeance. Wanting to give her the joy of her granddaughters during her chemo treatments, Karl and Julie packed up their girls and missionary weapons and returned to the States. Email and Internet posts sent after their return declared their new mission field was bright with hugs, laughter, wig swapping, soccer tournaments, barbeques, and merry car rides to and from the hospital. Joy was the high call of Christ in Karl and Julie's new mission field. They delivered it with gusto, love, and compassion.

As Christians, we must consider our responsibility to be missionaries. Like Julie and Karl, some of us are called to go farther away than others, give up more, and labor harder. Some of us can make cultural sacrifices; some cannot. But every single one of us can take on the Great Commission step by step, to our families, the lady looking for a good tomato at the produce bins, the teenager playing loud music, the youth with the gang tattoo, the people next to us in the doctor's office, or the guests at wedding receptions.

Jesus' calling to "be My witnesses " (Act 1:8) is to live the Great Commission wherever God places you. This is His training ground for worldwide missions. We must minister in everyday opportunities, home and abroad, solely for the purpose to be God's servant and give Him glory.

> "He who dwells in the secret place of the Most High
> shall abide under the shadow of the Almighty." (Psalm 91:1)

Welcome to YOUR Mission Field!

CONCLUSION
SEASON-STEPPING

Not being a numbers person, turning seventy-five this year forces me to face my nemeses. No matter which way I look at it, three quarters of a century is how long I've lived. This is cause, not for arithmetic, but reflection and intention. When I consider the years, I am astounded by the Creator who has orchestrated them. I can reflect clearly on seasons passed and God's truths weaved throughout.

> For everything there is a season, and a time
> for every matter under heaven. (Ecclesiastes 2:1)

Believe me, I was not as cavalier as Solomon, who penned those words, transitioning from season to season. The older I became, the harder I fought the changes of time. I wanted my life to continue the way I dreamed, with a permanent home, grandkids in and out, Sunday dinners with family, all things in order, and highlights rather than grey in my hair. I wanted to stay young, or at least youthful, and belong where I was rooted.

> (S)he is like a tree planted by streams of water that yields its fruit
> in its season, and its leaf does not wither. (Psalm 1:3)

Ah, but God knew there would be no fruit if I stayed put. So the new seasons rolled in. My husband retired, our daughter's family with five of our ten grandchildren moved away, we bought a forty-five-foot RV and chartered maps and began our travels away from home. The unexpected season of being a "Glamping Gypsy" was not my idea of "being planted by streams of water." Instead, we traveled from campground to campground all over the United States, immersing ourselves in the culture, scenery, and food in almost every state. Each time we broke camp (pulled the electric plug, unhitched the water hose, and pulled in the chocks), we said goodbye to friendly folks, then we drove to our next destination where we met and made more new friends.

What God wanted most for me, I believe, was not to nest at home but to embrace His magnificent Creation. With every mile, my roots spread deeper, and my fruit grew richer. It was a good season for my dried-up soul, and one I look forward to sharing with you, my patient and hardy readers, in a second edition of *Cutting and Pasting Truth*.

I realize now I have been "season stepping" with the LORD, His hand firmly around mine throughout the years. Today I am in a new season and am content though wary. Aren't we all a little suspect of serenity? Especially at my age. Trusting God's way and not mine through seasons of challenges, suffering, and transitions has had its benefits. Simply stated: God is ALWAYS good. I'm not wailing now as much as I used to and am finally learning to abide with Jesus. God's patience and perseverance for seventy-five years just show without a doubt, His steadfast Love. Obviously, numbers are not an issue with my Eternal Father!

Our new home in Florida is not on wheels, the warm weather soothes my raging joints, and despite COVID-19 and our years of wear and tear, my husband and I are well. This is no small blessing; it is a miracle every day. In this last quarter of my life on earth, however long it may be, I am walking with care and intention. What, I wonder, will be the essence of this season? I pray God will pour His wisdom, grace, and compassion into my fruit as I hold onto His promise that my "leaf will not wither" in the story that remains wholly His.

Bless the LORD O my soul, and all that is within me. Bless His holy name. Bless the LORD, O my soul, and forget not His benefits, who forgives all your iniquity, heals all your diseases, who redeems your life from the pit, who crowns you with steadfast love and mercy, who satisfies you with good so that your youth is renewed like the eagle's. (Psalm 103:1–5)

ABOUT THE AUTHOR

Meredith Bunting, formally called "Fluff Ball"—an endearment close to the mark—is prone to whimsy while bent to wisdom, drawn to emotion yet thrives in compassion, and besought with questions about purpose while remaining surprised by God's answers. Her driving passion is seeking the essence within the days given by God. A thirty-year battle with rheumatoid arthritis has rendered her joints weak, her hands deformed and her feet plain sore. This life-changing diagnosis, given to a former health and fitness professional, developed into a writing ministry, "Faith Fitness and Fruit," which demonstrates God's workout had higher goals than hers, which ultimately segued into writing devotionals that have been published internationally.

After traveling in a motorhome for months at a time, Meredith and her husband now live in their new home in Naples, Florida. They have three daughters and are blessed with ten grandchildren and one "best friend," Sophie, their Schnauzer.

A free ebook edition
is available with the
purchase of this book.

To claim your free ebook edition:

1. Visit MorganJamesBOGO.com
2. Sign your name CLEARLY in the space
3. Complete the form and submit a photo of the entire copyright page
4. You or your friend can download the ebook to your preferred device

Print & Digital Together Forever.

Snap a photo   Free ebook   Read anywhere

CPSIA information can be obtained
at www.ICGtesting.com
Printed in the USA
JSHW030025020222
22506JS00001B/4